The Message of the Rite

The Significance of Christian Rites of Passage

Roger Grainger

Lutterworth Press
Cambridge

FOR ROGER CRESSEY

Lutterworth Press
P.O. Box 60
Cambridge
CB1 2NT

British Library Cataloguing in Publication Data

Roger Grainger
The Message of the Rite
1. Christian church. Public worship
I. Title
264

ISBN 0-7188-2709-0

Copyright © Roger Grainger 1988

First published in 1988 by Lutterworth Press

Printed and bound in Great Britain
The Guernsey Press Co. Ltd., Guernsey, Channel Islands.

Contents

Note

This book has evolved from a study of patterns of corporate worship which I presented in 1983 to Geneva Theological College. The college requires that work presented by 'direct submission' should eventually be published. There is, however, another reason for publishing this. In his Introduction to my first book about ritual (*The Language of the Rite*, Darton, Longman & Todd, 1974) Professor David Martin commented that my explanation of the language of ritual tended to neglect 'its complex connections with the language of society'. This particular remark, in an otherwise friendly consideration of what I had written, has lain upon my mind for a decade. In this sequel to the original work I have tried to put things right.

Some of the material has already appeared in the form of articles in *New Blackfriars, New Fire, Worship,* and *Christian.* My thanks are due to the editors of these journals for the encouragement they have given me. I would also like to thank Anne Aliffe for typing the manuscript and Doreen Grainger for valuable help and invaluable inspiration.

Introduction

Christian ritual has suffered attacks from several directions, notably theology, psychopathology and anthropology. Protestant theologians in particular have regarded ritual as an idolatrous attempt on the part of men and women to reach God by means of human techniques and on human initiative. The attack is unjustified, however, for symbolic ritual candidly admits the real facts about mankind's way of understanding about God - that he can only really be approached by men and women who are willing to come completely out of the limitations of their own intellectual understanding and who would rather act out such a relationship than analyse it. A tendency in Reformation thinking would seem to suggest the opposite however: that thought is somehow able to leap the gap between mankind and God in a way that is denied to our physical nature, as though thinking were less earthly than moving about and doing things and men and women have a 'spiritual' - that is, an intellectual - identity which God prefers to their bodies because it is more in tune with his divine nature.[1] It is, of course, totally against the Judaeo-Christian understanding to confuse the intellect and the soul in such a way, and most Catholic Christians do not do it; or at least they try not to. The point is strongly made by creative liturgiologists such as Louis Bouyer and Herbert McCabe. Yet the attitude of mind that requires Christian initiation to be limited to those who are already fortunate enough to possess the right kind of cultural qualifications, who 'come from Christian homes and belong to Church families' approaches dangerously close to this kind of thing. The 'right' kind of social group and the 'proper' way of thinking about the world are very closely associated! Apart from this there is good reason to believe that the kind of intellectual understanding about God that is required as the rite's entrance fee actually proceeds from the rite itself; influenced by writers like Mary Douglas and Wayne Meeks some authorities lay stress on the idea that Christian teaching reflects ritual experience as much as it is reflected by it.[2]

Ritual has also been criticised from a psychological point of view.

Psychopathologists of the psychoanalytic school usually regard all ritual behaviour as neurotic, while behaviourism dismisses it as 'unadaptive' and consequently meaningless. For the psychopathologist, however, all rituals are essentially private. Corporate rites, says Freud, are merely a way of bypassing individual neuroses by institutionalising their symptoms. (Let's all be neurotic together!) However, as with a good deal of analytic thinking, this explanation is an attempt to make all the available evidence fit the original theory rather than to deal with the facts empirically. Freud does not say how a neurosis, which is essentially private or even secret, can conveniently be generalised in order to fulfil the demands of society. (It would surely be convenient if it could be, for neuroses are socially unacceptable whereas religion is not.) Psychoanalysis regards religion as essentially private, an extension of the self and its unconscious conflicts. It is particularly useful for individuals who, for one reason or another, perhaps because they have no adequate human father, are suffering from 'unresolved Oedipal conflict'; those who turn to God to satisfy needs that their own father did not. Such people seek a figure in which to locate the paternal characteristics of which they feel deprived. For Freud, religious belief is the answer for sexual anxiety; for Rank it is founded in man's unconscious fear of dying; only for Jung is it genuinely social.

Just as the ritual attacked by the Old Testament prophets was a dishonest manipulation of the cult, a way of distracting God's attention from the fact that his own people were engaged in disobeying his instructions with regard to their behaviour towards their fellow men and women, who were to be loved and respected in exactly the same way that he himself should be loved and respected, so the ritual criticised by psychologists is the same kind of antisocial distortion of the true nature of human rituals. The neurotic element in private ritual is just that: its privacy. The practice of corporate ritual is a function of being human and a proclamation about the social, relational and personal nature of our humanness.

The prophetic objection to ritual has frequently been misunderstood by Christians who, in the light of the imagery used by the writer of the Epistle to the Hebrews, should really have known better than to see Jesus's ministry in terms of an extended polemic against religious observances. Their attitude has drawn a good deal of support from a confusion about religion encouraged by nineteenth century anthropology, which persisted in regarding ritual as a kind of primitive science, an instrument for changing the nature of human reality by discovering ways of forcing

God's hand. This is to confuse religion with magic, which depends on the use of techniques that are essentially secret and must remain the property of the priest or shaman. It certainly does not make sense as a description of Christian sacramental experience, where what was once totally inaccessible, except to the few, is made perfectly available to all. The glory and the joy of Christian worship lies precisely here, in its proclamation of God's universal love, and its call to a responsiveness that is free, wholehearted and spontaneous. Because something is special it does not mean that it should be kept private. The Christian gospel leaves us in no doubt at all about this glorious fact, and Christian rites of passage are even more explicit. But again, there are those who take the common bread and the wine 'shed for many' and hedge it round with all sorts of social restrictions and ecclesiastical caveats. There are always those who invite us to draw near not by faith, but by special social and intellectual circumstances.

It is mainly from within the Church itself that corporate ritual has been attacked. Iconoclasm has been a powerful force in ecclesiastical history, and ritual is a kind of dramatised iconography. One cannot help wondering whether there might be a certain exclusiveness behind this pious horror of sensuality - after all the impact of this visual, aural, tactile, olfactory experience may produce an intensity of religious experience that is able to bypass the hierarchically arranged procedures for Church membership. Down the centuries the Church has set itself to guard 'the gate of Heaven', mediating immediacy to the unqualified. Humanly speaking this is an understandable aim - that is it fits in well with human psychology. But is it Christian?

As Christians we are called to surrender our own lives so that others may live. Surely, if this means anything it must involve letting others share in our precious discovery of new life within the rite and not hedging it about with all sorts of qualifications and restrictions. Our ritual is here, now, not eventually. We know this, and it terrifies us. We would rather cling to our defences, the barriers we erect around our ritual treasure.

Try as we may, we cannot enclose it. It evades our grasp. This is because it is essentially a gateway. The rite is the entrance to a new kind of life, a transformed kind of personhood, a new order of being. Within the rite men and women relate to one another in accordance with a new law, 'what I command you is to love one another'. Here the alienating selfishness of life lived in competition with others - a competition that no one can win because it is carried out at the expense of the life it grasps for - is transformed 'from love to love'. This is the perfection of order and meaning, the source and end of human fulfilment. In the rite men and women discover their true identity, their really personal names. The rite is concerned with the way we see ourselves and others, and consequently with our unique place within the order of society and the universe. This is why the rite has so much to offer to mankind and why it must be allowed to offer it. By analogy, Christian ritual is the demonstration of the personhood of God, who is also experienced as being present in the rite. It is the revelation of his name. As such it exposes the rebellious nature of all selfish organisation. It is as if the divine will reduces the lawlessness to order by naming it.

In this way, we are confirmed in our personhood every time we take part in the rite that calls us by name. This is particularly important at those times in our life when we pass from one stage of living to another. In a society in which everyone shared a single set of religious symbols important events in the lives of individuals could be given their underlying religious significance without undue difficulty, so that the people concerned could go on their way strengthened and refreshed by the experience of realising their true identity. Unfortunately, however, this is not the case with us. Our position is more of a missionary one. Certainly we must be aware of the need to pay attention to our own spiritual journeys, but we have an urgent need to proclaim Christ's message to the world, and a vital way in which we can do this is by inviting the world to share with us at the very heart of our mysteries. The human need for ritual, which comes to a climax at certain crucial times in our lives, presents the Church with a tremendous opportunity for evangelism in the widest and deepest sense of the word - a chance for outsiders to open themselves in body, mind and spirit to the transforming power of the Holy Spirit. Because on these occasions 'the world' still comes to us we are still in a position to welcome it into our family, if we will permit ourselves to be called to do so.

This is where the difficulty lies. We seem to want to keep such things to ourselves. Perhaps we resent the fact that we are only asked to perform this kind of office occasionally, when we ourselves are very sure that the price of sharing with us at these great personal festivals should be regular attendance at all our assemblies. Perhaps we resent the fact that our festivals are frequently used as ways of bestowing prestige of a non-theological kind within a wholly secular society. It seems wrong to us that people can simply come along when they need some kind of spiritual uplift without having really to believe, and certainly not to work at believing as we have to do. We feel that we are being used; worse, that God is being used.

The truth may be rather different, however. It is reasonable for the Church to object to the use of its rites by those who have no other contact with Christian belief, fellowship or worship. However, the unchurched do tend to be regarded in a negative way by churchgoers and this can be quite a barrier even before the subject of baptism has been broached at all. Here, as elsewhere, sociological factors come in the way of religious ones. Contrary to the opinions of many churchgoers, belief in God is very widespread; what many people object to is not Christianity but churchiness. Twentieth-century Western European society is secularist and agnostic, but this does not mean that the men and women who constitute it take no account of religious values or ignore their own religious feelings. What it does mean, however, is that individuals who opt for Church membership, of whatever denomination, may find themselves offending against social solidarity in ways unknown to earlier generations. The position of working-class people opting for the Church of England is a case in point; although anybody involving themselves too deeply in any worshipping community - even the Church of England - runs the risk of being considered a bit strange in a secularist society.

The conclusion must surely be that, in a society in which Church membership is socially divisive to an extent to which during the last few centuries at least, it has rarely been, 'outsiders' deserve to be made as welcome as possible, or at least to be given the benefit of the doubt and not made to feel second-class Christians. Anybody who is willing to take the step - and it can be a daunting one - of 'going to see the vicar' needs all the support and encouragement they can receive. He - or she - will certainly have strong feelings about the matter, feelings which may well be genuinely religious.

At least the first steps have been taken, whatever may happen afterwards. As the Psalmist says: 'Taste and see ...' The mystery must be shared. It cannot simply be talked about. Which is why, first of all, it must be made available.

1

Identity and Social Change

We live in a rapidly changing world. This is only a cliché because it is so obviously true. In order to survive we must be reminded of its truth as often as possible. Unfortunately, to use another cliché, familiarity breeds contempt, expressed in this case by a kind of fatalistic resignation: 'there's nothing I can do about it, is there?' It is not that we are against change - indeed we often enjoy it - but we prefer it to happen at our own speed. We certainly do not like to be overtaken by the kind of changes over which we have no control, so that we are left feeling that we are not so much involved in change, which can be a creative experience for us, but are the victims of events originating far beyond ourselves. We do not like it to happen too often, or too quickly. Meanwhile, the tempo of social change continues to increase and the directions that it takes diversify and multiply. The individual, caught up in a maelstrom of unexpected events, can only echo Joxer's immortal words in Juno and the Paycock 'the whole world's in a state of chassis'. It is important to realise that this is not simply a subjective impression. The informed opinion of historians, archaeologists, economists, sociologists and psychologists suggests that rapidly accelerating social change is an objective fact. Almost twenty years ago Kenneth Boulding, an American economist, pointed out that 'The world of today ... is as different from the world in which I was born as that world was from Julius Caesar's. I was born in the middle of human history. Almost as much has happened since I was born as before.'[1]

Boulding was concerned about changes at the deepest social and economic level, genuine historical transformations of the fabric of society, and not with the kaleidoscope variety of fashionable crazes that characterised the decade in which he himself wrote; but the shifting patterns that occur on the surface of social life represent another and almost equally important source of confusion and unease to individual men and women. In the second half of the twentieth century cultural change is not only rapid but ephemeral, and there is an intimate relationship between social structure and individual frames of reference. A society that changes at every level of organisation with increasing rapidity and, at the same time, appears to shift backwards and forwards without rhyme or reason, provides a most uncomfortable setting for personal reflection about the fundamental nature and final significance of human life. No wonder that more and more people prefer to suspend their judgement about such matters and that those who claim that human history has some kind of underlying or overarching meaning and purpose tend to stand out amongst their fellows as disturbing non-conformists who must give an account of their social eccentricity or be regarded as potentially dangerous sectarians.

Nor is it any wonder that an increasing number of people become seriously disturbed at the psychological level and need some kind of specialised psychiatric help in order to deal with the confusion that exists 'inside themselves'. At the most fundamental level the human organism and its environment cannot realistically be separated from each other. In any investigation into the nature of human experience, whether biological or psychological, the primary subject matter must always be the organism's life within its environment. This is obviously true when we think about it. How can we claim to understand anything at all if we ignore its context? There is in fact no function of any animal, human or otherwise, that may be realistically defined or scientifically assessed except as a characteristic of its total life experience.

Students of human and animal behaviour are coming more and more to recognise that both psychologically and physiologically the self that perceives and the things that it perceives, whether these are people, animals and objects, or ideas about them, belong together and must be considered together. Indeed, subject and object may only be separated by regarding them in the abstract; and this abstraction from the reality of living experience has provided a distraction from scientific accuracy ever since Descartes asserted that the human organism's ability to produce such abstractions was the single supremely important datum about our existence.

For those who find themselves victims of a world in which as a result of chaotic social changes they can no longer see their way forward the problem is much more than one of scientific accuracy. It is the basic dilemma of how to be at all, when the ground of being has lost all sense of

permanence and the very foundations upon which the self is constructed are subject to periodic tremors of an unpredictable kind. In
such a world as this, upon what can I depend? Upon what can I build
my life? If our experience of ourselves and our understanding of everything else that exists for us are so inextricably intertwined, the need
to make sense of an endless succession of contradictory ideas about the
nature of reality by organising them into a consistent view of life, can
impose an intolerable strain on our 'psychological homeostasis' - seriously, and in some cases, permanently, interfering with our ability to
achieve peace of mind. The result may be what the gestalt psycho-
therapists call 'a discrepancy between the verbal concept of the self
(that is, our attempts to talk ourselves out of perceptual difficulties)
and the felt awareness of the self',[2] in other words, neurosis.

Whether or not the effect of social change is as dramatic as this is
open to question, of course. Not everyone who lives in a social setting like
ours cracks under the strain. However, it may well be that the feeling of
personal alienation induced by extended exposure of these conditions
does have a harmful effect on us at a very deep spiritual level. For instance,
in a rapidly changing world we may become frightened of establishing
close personal relationships. Who could blame us if we did? When
everything is so uncertain, how can we afford to take chances with our
most precious and personal possession, our own self? Who knows what
might happen? Our natural human timidity about taking risks that are
likely to affect the rest of our lives is reinforced by our experience of the
things going on around us. Besides, if we cannot trust the world, can we
really trust ourselves? We may think we know what we are doing, where
we are going, but how can we possibly be sure? Better to play safe, and
'keep ourselves to ourselves'.

At least, it seems better. In fact, the exercise is almost totally self-
defeating. To try to avoid the personal risks involved in living is to try to
avoid being alive at all. In Tillich's marvellous phrase, it is 'avoiding non-
being by avoiding being'.[3] And this, at last, is the very heart of our
dilemma. We can only defend ourselves from risks by protecting ourselves from people. To do this is to isolate ourselves from the source of our
personal wholeness, the very source of ourselves. The courage to be as a
separate self actually originates in our willingness to be part of something
greater than ourself. We cannot use our own individuality defensively and
get away with it, because the only way that individuality thrives is in its
relationship with others. We become ourselves as we grow more able to
contemplate our unity with other selves. No one has expressed this better

than Martin Buber: in turning towards the Other, 'being is disclosed to us'.[4]

In relationship we turn away from ourselves towards the other person. It is only when we do this that we discover who we really are. It is as if the other person alone has the power to reveal us to ourselves. This startling fact is only surprising, however, if we leave God out of our thinking and assume that we are responsible for ourselves, our own existences. The life we draw from God is a life that he bestows on all his creatures. It is a life of shared personhood, an ultimate regard for and from the Other. It is because we have become separated from the source of our life and the ground of our being that we feel ourselves so threatened by 'the changes and chances of this mortal world'. Every systematical religion throughout the world has its own version of the event, but for each the shape of the primal scenario tends to remain the same. The relationship between creator and creature, heaven and earth, is perpetually under strain, and the source of weakness is always on the side of man rather than the side of God. How could it be otherwise, while men and women are faced with the necessity of reconciling two contradictory kinds of idea about life - on the one hand that everything is subject to change, nothing is permanent, least of all the individual self; and on the other, that everything has a final meaning, a reality and integrity that is changeless by definition? Our senses tell us one thing, as we see, hear, touch, taste and feel the world about us, and our behaviour proclaims the other, as we direct all our energies towards making sense of all the contradictory information we receive from them. In every one of life's emergencies a religious man or woman will turn towards God for a solution which is inclusive, stable, and established in permanence. Whatever else he may be, God is always and inescapably the one who holds everything together, because he is the only one who holds the answers to life's problems. The anthropologist Clifford Geertz puts this very clearly:

There are at least three points where chaos ... threatens to break in upon man: at the limits of his analytic capacities, at the limits of his powers of endurance, and at the limits of his moral insight. Bafflement, suffering and a sense of intractable ethical paradox are all, if they become intense enough or are sustained long enough, radical challenges to the proposition that life is comprehensible and that we can, by taking thought, orient ourselves effectively within it - challenges with which any religion, however 'primitive', that hopes to persist, must somehow attempt to cope.[5]

Society itself, of course, is one way in which we attempt to come to terms with the pressure to find answers to intractable problems of life and death. Social structures have been described as attempts to 'impose a meaningful order, or nomos, upon the discrete experiences and meanings of individuals'.[6] Sociologists have often drawn attention to the similarity between social awareness and religious faith, because both exert a powerful influence upon the individual in the direction of a greater personal involvement in the affairs of the community. People who share one's own interpretation of life's meaning and purpose underline one's own sense of reality, and also of the social reality to which one belongs. Religion is seen as a kind of glue for binding societies together: the more people adhere to it, the stronger it becomes and so the more people adhere to it, etc. The need for stability in human affairs itself creates a superordinate source of social stability, 'a sacred time within which merely human history is but an episode'.[7]

Obviously, this kind of argument provides a very incomplete account of what religion actually does for human beings. It really only shows us what happens when society and religion become confused, to the detriment of both. However, it is a useful reminder that the action of our own religious awareness upon the society in which we live is to a certain extent reflexive, so that the way in which we translate our craving for meaning and order into actual religious behaviour may be powerfully affected by the presuppositions inherent in the particular society in which we happen to live. (An example would be the actions performed in the name of God by the Spanish Inquisition.) No doubt societies influence religions, just as religions affect societies; but this does not mean that they are the same thing, or even the same kind of thing. It may be true that they derive from the same instinct for meaning and could perhaps be regarded as different ways of approaching the problem of satisfying it: not mutually exclusive ways (this is clearly demonstrated by the presence of religiously inclined individuals and groups in social settings where the dominant philosophy of life is humanistic or even atheistic), but certainly not identical ones, either. After all, it was the need to rebel against official 'social' meanings and follow a wholly personal vision, a uniquely individual revelation of the truth about God and man, that brought saints to the scaffold and drove the Christian Fathers into the desert.[8]

It is precisely at this point that the attempt by modern sociologists to 'explain' God as the product of our need for wholeness and order in society fails - by ignoring the contrast between the world of religious faith, the ideal condition to which believers aspire, and the ordinary arrangements that society makes for the daily lives of men and women. The difference is in fact crucial. As Robert Browning puts it, this is 'what Heaven's for'. Thus our religious awareness is at one and the same time hyper-personal and meta-social. It is experienced as originating in the depths of an individual's personal and private being yet it takes in the whole universe and beyond. It is not simply something learned from others as part of a formal educational process, for it breaks up as many societies, and as many families, as it unites. It seems obvious enough that the impulse to seek some kind of personal relationship with the source of divine perfection is not the same thing as the need to live in an ordered society and cannot possibly be reduced to this. Indeed, only a fool would confuse the City of God with the efforts of social planners, however enlightened. In fact, however, those who think like this are not really as foolish as they seem to be; they are simply well-meaning observers, doing their best to take a detached 'scientific' view of processes that do not lend themselves very easily to be normal methods of social analysis. It is certainly true that rational thought about religion is no substitute for the personal encounter with divinity. In the actual moment of encounter, the other is more other than we had surmised. Too other, in fact, for our intellectual comfort. To experience God's perfection at first hand is not to be instructed but transformed.

It is at this primal, precognitive level that the relationship between human vulnerability, human transience and divine permanence is to be approached. The need to bring the shifting world of men and women into the presence of God's 'eternal changelessness' is indeed an instinctive one. Certainly the individual man, woman or child needs to live in a secure and stable social environment and suffers considerably when the comfort given by the presence of familiar people and recognisable events is removed: but at the crisis of our lives we seek a more secure refuge than this.

This is not only so of those of us who are overtly 'religious'. It may well be that the awareness of God works most powerfully to influence our life at an unconscious level as well as a conscious one. Certainly, all human experience seems to possess a fundamental religious dimension. C.G. Jung describes how, at the level of the 'collective unconscious', individual awareness ceases to function in any kind of exclusive or individualistic sense so that, in fact, all mankind participates in a primal experience of being, a precognitive wholeness and completeness in which separate existences are no longer self-conscious because the only kind of awareness is God-consciousness. If this is the case, then everyone on earth is a religious person. When we deny this fact, as most of us do from time to time, even those of us who lay claim to a particular religious affiliation, we suffer a painful distortion of our psychic experience. The demand of God is for complete self-acceptance at all our psychic levels, which means an ability to live with our submerged spirituality as well as with the preoccupations of consciousness. To surrender to God's demand requires a determined effort of the will, because it cuts directly across cherished beliefs about individual autonomy and threatens to undermine the conscious structures of our personality that we have so painstakingly erected in order to be able to deal with the ordinary pressures of life in the world. Nothing that threatens from this quarter is to be compared to the pressure upon us of the divine demand that we should genuinely acknowledge all the implications of our own individual mortality and willingly accept our share in the underlying religious identity of humankind.[9]

Perhaps we do not need 'depth psychology' to tell us this, however. Jung's analysis of human experience certainly accords well with the biblical understanding about mankind's relationship with God as revealed in Christ. The idea of a 'denied truth' that distorts our ordinary everyday experience of living and causes us to search for salvation in the wrong place should certainly strike a chord in Christian hearts. Because we will not learn what we already know, unconsciously, about God, even we tend to find our own 'reasonable' excuses for the distress that afflicts us by taking refuge in neurotic conditions, which provide us with 'a substitute for legitimate suffering'.[10] There is no substitute, says Jung, for the willingness of men and women to face the source of their confusion, which lies at the point where two worlds meet, the world of their primal belonging and that of their self-imposed exile from the source of life. So long as we strive to devote ourselves entirely to the latter sphere, the former remains distorted and terrifying, an alien country we dare not let ourselves venture into for fear of losing our hard-won sense of direction. Those who are able to visit it, either by the medium of dreams, or by taking as guide one who has redeemed and restored every human experience return infinitely restored and renewed.

The form taken by this fundamental symbolism is often the *mandala*, or 'magic circle', representing 'a primordial image of psychic totality'. 'The Mandala appears spontaneously as a compensatory archetype, bringing order, showing the possibility of order'.[11] This is a symbol of the *coincidentia oppositorum*, or the transformation of opposites into a higher synthesis: 'Whenever this symbol, which can manifest itself in the most divergent forms, makes its appearance the balance between the ego and the unconscious is restored.'[12] As 'the archetype of inner order' the mandalas represent the relationship between two unities, the divine and the human, which image itself constitutes a super-ordinate unity. In the dreams of people who are in the grip of an existential crisis, or in the 'imaginary fantastical drawings' of patients undergoing psychotherapy, it occurs in the shape of 'the QUADRATURA CIRCULI, the square on the circle or the circle in the square'[13] - an age old religious emblem which goes back to prehistoric times and 'combines the imagery of separation with the imagery of mutuality' within a single structure. Indeed, we have only to glance at the religions of the world to be amazed at how often the image recurs. Whatever the specific doctrine may be, the mandala's message is the same - healing is available for the wounded and incomplete, divine wholeness for individual souls.

It is worth noting, however, that the kind of dreams that captured Jung's attention were those which occur at times in our personal lives when it is hardest to think clearly about what is happening to us: periods of transition and painful personal change. When our conscious understanding fails to provide us with any kind of satisfactory answer to the problems that beset us, our dreams may mediate an awareness of divine order and perfection. At such times confidence comes to us from the recognition of a certainty infinitely greater and more potent than that which is available to our rational thought, a truth from which rationality proceeds but one that is in no way dependent on the conclusions at which it arrives.

Jung, then, tells us a good deal about the nature of religious awareness: that it subsists in a vision of perfection that unites conflicting elements within a mysterious harmony, that it is fundamental to our nature, mysterious in identity, closely associated with and in total contrast to ordinary secular consciousness; and that it inspires and liberates us while establishing us more firmly and securely within our own true identity as human beings. God's message to men and women about the meaning of what happens in human life - for example those events in history that are central to Christian understanding - lies outside his brief. What is also missing, from a Christian point of view, is any indication of God's marvellous activity in the world in the form of direct personal action; action involving the painful surrender of personhood for the purpose of giving life to others. In other words, although analytical psychology can affirm the transforming power of religion, it cannot tell us how to receive this power into our conscious lives because it does not know, officially that is, in whose name it is bestowed.

However collective its significance, this name is personal, and the various means of communication associated with it are personal too. The union with God is offered to individuals who are invited home to share in a belonging that, we are assured, was ours from the beginning. The invitation comes to particular persons in circumstances that underline their particularity, circumstances that cause them to wonder why it should happen to them, of all people - a particularly prodigal son, or adulterous woman.... And the invitations are by name, for each of us is called to share and called to be him or herself.

Having a 'valid' personal name is of profound importance. Psychologically speaking, one's own name is one's most precious possession. It is the certificate of our membership of human society, our passport to the country inhabited by the rest of the human race. It is the way in which we are recognised and acknowledged by other people as ourselves, the key word in the language of social belonging and consequently, of personal belonging. In communities where the sense of corporate belonging is strong and the 'nomos', by which I mean the criteria of social belonging constituting a community's identity, is well established, an individual's own name is more precious than ever. It represents a particular position within a closely knit network of names, so that to deny a name is literally to refuse to acknowledge a place in society. In situations in which human existence is perceived as directly congruent with societal status - for example in some of the tribal societies described by anthropologists - the ritualised removal of a personal name can be viewed as a kind of death sentence. Not only this, but, from the earliest recorded times, to deliver one's personal name into the hands of someone who does not himself share society's nomos has been considered to be something to be avoided at all costs, probably because the effect of this is to let a stranger into society without receiving the authority of the nomos. In doing this one has admitted him or her into society 'through the back door' as it were, so running the risk of powerful sanctions on the part of society against oneself. Even in more developed societies this principle remains the same. As Emile Durkheim pointed out, for an individual human being to lose the social acceptability - the social meaning - of his or her name is tantamount to being bereft of a feeling of personal worth. In fact, Durkheim uses the term 'anomie', or absence of identification with social norms, to describe a condition of society in which the bonds that tie the individual members together are too loose to give people any real sense of social belonging. 'Normlessness', 'anomie', the social 'nomos', are all ways of describing the peculiar value and significance of individual names that are authentically social and, consequently, fully personal.[14]

The Christian Church still functions in order to give men and women a valid personal name. It does this not only in Holy Baptism but in every one of the ceremonies, sacramental or otherwise, that constitute rites of passage within Christianity, each of which is a kind of baptism in the sense of being a means of establishment within personhood. Thus, in modern secular society, the Church performs a vital symbolic function in countering 'anomie' in a loosely knit - some would even say a disintegrating - society for those who are willing to attribute spiritual authority to it. To this extent the Church continues to give society a name, for as the public identity and the personal experience of individuals changes when they take on new social roles during the course of their lives - joining society, undertaking adult responsibility within it, preparing to contribute new members to it and finally leaving it - the Church reinforces in them a sense of their suitability for those roles and of the dignity and propriety of the roles themselves. It could even be said that this ability to give individuals a name that will carry them through life - to give it to them and from time to time remind them of it - is the most effective means of evangelism that the Christian Church possesses.

This is not to say, of course, that membership of the Christian Church depends on the reception of an officially recognised 'Christian name'. The name bestowed at baptism is much less tangible, and much more important than this. It may be described as participation in a particular kind of personhood; not a sign of participation but participation itself. It is Christ's personhood, his name, that is taken, and any human naming derives its religious significance from this alone. The symbol of a relationship rather than any kind of thing or possession, this name confirms us in personhood because it establishes us in our true life, the life of giving and receiving, at the most important level. Adult baptismal candidates need not change their 'ordinary' name, the one they are generally known by, in order to receive a 'special' one, because the ordinary becomes special in accordance with the sacramental principle of divine participation that is at work here. It is this transformation of ordinary meanings, and particularly of the meaning of personhood itself,

that exerts an influence upon the unchurched, attracting them to sacramental services and rites of passage. At least, it is this as much as the
desire to achieve some kind of alternative social identity. They do not
seek another name so much as divine validation of the one they already
have.[15]

This may go some way towards explaining the particular role that
the Church plays in this country as the guardian of people's social identity.
Generally speaking the Church is considered to be benevolent, even warm
hearted. In many places, the ancient missionary strategies have left us with
an ecclesiastical structure that has ensured a close geographical identification between clergy and population. The parson's role as individual
counsellor and spokesman for the local community has provided an
invaluable link between those who attended church and those who did not.
Since the Reformation the involvement of the clergy with an identifiable
form of domesticity has made it less practicable to maintain the barriers
between a priestly caste and the rest of humanity. The presence of 'the
vicar' - and even 'the curate' - as part of the daily scene in village and
town, or on the new housing estate, has made the appearance of clergy
familiar to almost everyone, not simply those who on Sunday mornings
make up the congregation of the faithful. The clergy are considered to be
friendly, generally speaking, and their friendliness is valued and appreciated: 'I don't go to church myself, but I've nothing against our man.' Our
man is local, he belongs to us. Our man, our church. The church is valued
as being indigenous, part of the country, part of being English. Thus, in an
important sense, the non-churchgoer identifies with the parish church. He
does not go, but he knows the vicar, and has an aunt who goes, so in a way,
it is 'in the family'. If anything should happen to the church building: if it
should be declared redundant and closed, he is among the first to protest,
even though his own absence may have been a contributing factor. 'We
know where you are, if we want you' he tells the vicar. You could say that
the presence of the familiar building, and what it represents in the way of
security and stability, of the 'rightness' of things, contributes in an
important way to his sense of identity.

Unfortunately, the Church's tendency to discount the deep psychological significance of its name-bestowing rituals and to use them as
celebrations of human ability to conform to the rules of a particular social
group rather than as gateways into a way of being in which we are more
able to experience the reality of God within the human soul has meant that
the intellectually impossible meeting, the life that is pure gift, has become
more and more the prerogative of the few. The ritual has become the right

of those who satisfy the specific requirements of membership even before they ask for it, so that for some the impossible is an earned possibility, a technique possessed by a particular sect. 'At present,' says André Laurentin, 'everything is in the hands of a sacerdotal "caste" ';[16] and Tissa Balasuriya complains that 'the Eucharist, founded on a deep re-interpretation by Christ of the Exodus ... has become domesticated and privatised'.[17] The tragedy is that society is in fact willing to listen to the Church, but it needs the Church's understanding. In all its diversity of opinions and attitudes, its confusion of individual voices, it must first of all be embraced if it is to be centred in and focussed upon God. As Laurentin puts it 'The liturgy will find its resurrection from the dead when the whole living world is found in it.'

The Church tends to use its rites of passage as barriers rather than gateways: only such and such kinds of people can be baptised, married, buried, remembered, in church. This happens, though, because the Church tends to underestimate ritual anyway; or rather it respects its theological meaning and its ecclesiastical significance while misunderstanding its psychological, and sociological, functions. This rejection of ritual is no isolated phenomenom, but reflects a movement in contemporary thinking that dislikes structures *per se*, and tends to regard them as enemies of 'freedom' and 'spontaneity' and hence of genuine relationship. Societies cannot dispense with structures any more than human beings can do without their bodies; to deny the need of men and women to organise relationships is to deny reality itself and to start thinking in a dangerously schizoid way. In 1974 I wrote a book about religious ritual in which I made the claim that, far from being inhibited or repressed by organised action, human freedom actually emerges from structure and is seriously or even tragically limited by our refusal to take account of this fact.[18] Wherever there are people there are rules governing their relationship and to misunderstand these 'structures of interaction' or deliberately ignore them is to court disaster. Structures only inhibit relationships and limit freedom when the necessity for them is not understood or acknowledged. The Church's traditional use of ritual to proclaim its own identity and bestow identity on others is the living proof of its acceptance of the fundamental significance of ritual as a mode of direct relationship with Christ himself.

For Christians ritual remains the uniquely revealing phenomenon, and to understand this we have to realise the value of ritual as ritual, for it is not a matter of what it signifies, but of what it is. It signifies itself. To borrow McLuhan's famous phrase, here the medium really is the message. Ritual is a pronouncement about man's human identity that takes the form of a practical demonstration of what it really means to be a structured spirit, an incarnate soul. For those who would communicate the reality of the truth enshrined in the Christian gospels ritual is literally irreplaceable, for it presents men and women in the actions of life, the change and interchange of human relationship in which we meet as strangers and recognise one another as fellows. It is from the initial meeting symbolised in the rite that our life as persons proceeds. In reminding us over and over again of this fact ritual performs a vital function, for once the need for definite models of human interaction is acknowledged again, structure may regain the necessary confidence to be open and candid about itself; and once it is candid, relationship follows as the result of genuine meeting.

Ritual is indispensable to the Church for it is the living sign language of the human soul. Bodily movement and spiritual intention are united here as nowhere else within the realm of interpersonal communication. The result is a message about being human that possesses an irresistible force, clarity and directness, for the human body has a realism that no idea can ever have. In rituals we show our willingness to back up our aspirations with our very selves, to 'lay on the line' our own bodies. Not simply to think about service, but actually to perform the actions of love. The human body is the personal gift that carries its own guarantee, because it is the sole human possession that having once been given away can never be taken back again; which is why actions have a significance that thought or intention alone can never possess. An action once performed can never be wholly denied. It is not simply an idea that can be rationalised away or adapted retrospectively to suit changed circumstances. To change the situation requires another action. This is true of things done privately (if anything at all is ever really private) and it is doubly true of the self-conscious intention of ritual. For good or ill, rituals 'stick'. They are not forgotten or denied but constitute points in our personal experience that are unique, occasions when a particular intention has been well and truly registered, a position unequivocally established; moments of stillness within the flux of time when we pause and say 'this is what I mean, this is how I am'. We say it here and now, not only to ourselves but to other people and to God. Saying it we find out who we are.

The way into this kind of involvement is by means of the rite itself. Each experience of corporate Christian ritual is a 'journey into the interior of the Faith' and may itself actually induce faith by its ability to integrate feeling with thought, shaping the emotions that belong to human relationship in accordance with the vision of an overarching meaning, one that is founded in our original and final relationship with God himself.

2

Ritual and Anomie

What I have been saying about society in general, tends not to be true about certain well-defined groups within it. In fact, of course, it is the general truth that defines the particular exceptions. During the last 100 years the fundamental religious awareness of mankind has been focussed within a multiplicity of groups that assert the primacy of the spiritual very forcibly. It could be said that the danger here might lie in a neglect of those psychic functions that take account of the physical organism, namely sensation and intuition; but the life of faith has flourished. These developments have been comprehensively described elsewhere.[1]

Generally speaking, however, in modern secular society the expression of the religious nomos tends to be diffused over a wide range of activities and projects of a social nature, each of which expresses a deep concern for and involvement with personal relationship without claiming to be explicitly religious. At the same time there are areas of ordinary life in which the nomos stands out extremely clearly in all its original identity as the emblem of an awareness that is unashamedly theological. In other words, some of the things that happen to people even today remind them of their ecclesiastical loyalties in ways they find difficult to ignore. Important changes in life and their associated psychological traumas bring home to us the terms of our relationship with God and the world. By straining the cords that bind us to the truth that sustains us, the truth of our created being, they remind us very forcibly of the presence of these cords. The importance of ritual at such times can be literally crucial.

Religious rituals project the imagery of wholeness and balance in order to induce in us the presence of a psycho-spiritual unity and repose. As acted symbol rather than theoretical propositions, they are movements, gestures and words of timeless significance happening in a place that is set apart and yet central. Rites give shape and clarity to human experience by

focussing divine revelation and giving it an unforgettable explicitness at
the most fundamental level of human awareness. What cannot be captured
by thought is incorporated in an event, as vulnerable individuals present
themselves to the one who calls them to himself and one another. Ritual
does not simply represent society in the sense of expressing social feeling
and corporate religious aspiration, it creates society because it draws upon
a source of unity that is not available to the conscious awareness of
individual members of a group. This is a unity of being that is participated
in at an unconscious level, but experienced by consciousness as a reaching
out in faith towards the other. It is an absence that is made into a presence
by the quality of a shared intention to worship. It is as if the action of
focussing our intention upon God moves us in powerful ways towards the
creation of communities. More will be said about this later. First of all it
is important to take account of some of the results of this phenomenon as
they occur in the life of groups of people who benefit most strikingly from
corporate ritual, sections of society whose experience of life in the world
makes them very conscious of the value of ritual as a way of discovering
their own social - and consequently personal - identity.

Strangers and Exiles
People sometimes suffer rejection at the hands of society because they are
expatriates: on the other hand, they may become expatriates because of
some kind of social stigma bestowed on them within the country from
which they are in exile. This kind of alienation tends, however, to work
both ways. Its effect on individuals and groups may be a paradoxical one.
Such 'displaced persons' cling strongly to the very things that symbolise
their distance from the wider society. The role of religion, and particularly
religious ritual, in cases like this is most immediately in the establishment
of a recognisable group identity. To belong to God is to participate in a
reality infinitely wider, stronger and more inclusive than any human social
structure; and a community founded on such a basis, one that unashamedly
proclaims its divine nature and origins, immediately establishes its unique
identity over and against vaguer and less specific social philosophies, or
ideologies of a determinedly atheistic kind. To proclaim one's membership of the Christian Church in circumstances like these is to 'sing the
Lord's song in a strange land'. From a psychological point of view it is a
song well worth singing.
        Studies of the incidence of psychological illness among expatriate
populations show that members of immigrant groups are more likely to
develop psychiatric conditions than people who stay at home in their own

country. This has been explained in terms of social alienation caused by
the difficulty in adjusting to changes in both the social and the material
conditions of life, and the psychological stresses involved in the encounter
with an environment that must seem disturbingly or even frighteningly
alien: 'culture shock', in fact. In drawing attention to this, Anthony Clare[2]
reports that, out of all the immigrants who have been studied, the only
people who appear to be unaffected are the Irish expatriates now living in
London - the community referred to as the Bog Irish by Mary Douglas.[3]
Not only are these Irish Catholics psychologically healthier than other
immigrant populations in Britain, they are actually less prone to mental
illness than the people they left behind in Southern Ireland. Dr Clare
confesses that he is not able to explain why this should be the case; why
these particular people should be the sole exception to what appears to be
a general rule about the culturally dispossessed.

Dr Douglas suggests an answer. It is, she says, because, even more
religiously than their kinfolk back in the Republic, they go to Mass. They
cling tenaciously to their corporate identity as this is established and
proclaimed in rites of religious belonging; public pronouncements about
the existence of a divine order that is able to establish and confirm them
in authentic personhood. Even more than most members of the divine
society of the Church, the Bog Irish know precisely why they go to Mass.

Patients and Prisoners
Expatriates of the kind just described are usually, although of course not
always, voluntary exiles. If by any chance the effect of cultural trauma
should be to contribute to some kind of psychiatric breakdown in an
individual, he or she is likely to become an exile of another kind. Being
admitted into hospital has a radically disruptive effect on our ordinary
patterns of living. Like a surgical operation even a short stay in hospital
severs the tissue of events and expectations and contributes to a movement
of defensive withdrawal in which each individual patient clings to his or
her own area of physical and psychological autonomy: my bed-space; my
locker; and eventually my ward; my body and mind; my history; my
illness. It is characteristic of the human species, along with other animals,
to defend its territory and repel invaders. The hospital merely creates a
situation in which the awareness of vulnerability reaches new peaks of
intensity: my life, my death....

In a general hospital the symbol of this state of affairs is the
operating theatre, or the surgeon's scalpel. In psychiatric hospitals it tends
to be the huge institutional structure itself which signifies the rape of

personality most vividly. That and the terrifying implication of madness, a condition of being in which it is taken for granted that I can no longer properly understand the meaning communicated by my own or other people's thought and feelings. It is for this reason, I must realise, that my freedom is limited by being confined to bed when I feel physically fit and by having my clothes taken away as part of my initiation into an alien world of professional healers who 'know more about me than I do about myself'. In every kind of hospital the depersonalising assumptions of 'scientific medicine' reduce men and women to a condition of child-like dependence in which the contributing subject is regarded as the passive object of someone else's expertise. In this highly specialised environment human ingenuity appears to be rigorously directed towards the dual purpose of cancelling out the effects of breakdown and disguising its presence as an unavoidable characteristic of the human condition. Despite their explicit purpose of healing, the technological self-assurance of a modern hospital may give the impression that its intention is to safeguard society from a truth about itself which it has every intention of forgetting - the presence of a terrifying vulnerability. By isolating one kind of pathology in order to concentrate on its eradication, another kind of sickness is produced in men and women, one whose effects are even more destructive. Michael Wilson has called the hospital 'a place of truth'.[4] To a very real extent the hospital's truth is identical with the prison's. Both hospitals and prisons are 'cradled in anxiety':[5] the anxiety is the truth, and the truth the anxiety.

In prisons and hospitals many of the things that gave life shape are removed from people, so that they are faced with the task of discovering a new set of structural elements around which to organise their perception of the world. For hospital patients the need to redefine their role is the natural result of becoming ill and having to depend on other people for a whole range of things, both tangible and intangible, that they were formerly able to do for themselves at their own speed and in their own way. On the other hand, there is no doubt that in hospitals as in prisons the restriction of an individual's personal horizon is the implicit (specially contrived) consequence of our attitude to intractable social situations of any kind, physical, emotional or legal - the urge to keep such things well away from ourselves, preferably by making proper revisions of their containment 'outside the camp'.

The consequence of this is that hospital patients, like prison inmates, enjoy the ambiguous consolation that comes from fellowship in adversity. In general hospitals this solidarity is mainly attributable to physical and emotional vulnerability, the pervading presence of sickness and death. In prisons and psychiatric hospitals it is largely the result of stigma.

This is not the whole story, however. There is a deeper source of personal unity than either the perceptual integrity that we associate with habit and expectation or the comradeship that comes from enforced membership of a beleaguered minority group. There is a peace of mind that can only come from the awareness of ultimate causes and final purposes. The experience of religious men and women both in hospital and prison bears witness to the presence of a spiritual focus, a kind of metaphysical lodestone for disorientated feelings and ideas. There do not appear to be any official statistics about church and chapel attendances in either prisons or hospitals. I can only quote my own experience, which is that in fifteen years of travelling round hospital wards the number of people to whom I have spoken who have claimed to have no religious feelings of any kind could be counted on the fingers of one hand. This state of affairs is reflected in the number of people who receive Holy Communion: out of 900 patients in the hospital where I am a chaplain, nearly 100 ask for Communion each week. This compares strikingly with the available statistics for people outside hospital. It is a psychiatric hospital, certainly, and therefore untypical of hospitals in general; but there is no evidence that religious people are more prone to mental illness than anyone else.

These men and women do not claim to be 'religious', and a high proportion of them do not usually attend church outside hospital. Certainly, their action could be considered to be the result of a desperate determination to 'try anything once'. I do not think that this is usually the case. Rather, it is an instinctive move towards acknowledging a fact of their own experience of which, up to now, they have declined for one reason or another to take very much notice. It is as if being in hospital has brought things to a head for them, so that a whole dimension of their lives, what might be called their innate spirituality, is able to come out of the shadows and be consciously recognised as a vital part of their personhood, something that demands integration with the rest of their personalities if they are to receive true healing. God has shown himself to them in the breaking of their lives.

In all this, the part played by ritual is of great importance. It is the imagery of religion as the symbolism of a perfect belonging that exerts so much fascination for individuals beset by the crippling sense of their own loneliness and vulnerability. Ritual 'works' in situations where argument is futile and exhortation useless if not downright counterproductive. On the acute ward of a psychiatric hospital, for example, human defensiveness tends to be at its highest and most impenetrable. Ritual, however, exists primarily in the action itself, forestalling argument and postponing reflection, while having a profound effect upon all our subsequent thought. This is why it can be so appropriate in situations when ordinary human dialogue is impossible or impractical, because people are too frightened, too depressed or simply too ill to be reached in any other way.

Bereaved People
Peter Speck writes:

From birth to death we experience many losses, whether actual or threatened, and our reaction to them influences the character we develop and the attitudes we form ... the loss may be of an object, a limb, an organ, a person or a relationship, and clearly some losses will represent a much bigger threat to our well-being than others.[6]

We have been looking very briefly at some experiences of loss: loss of ethnic or cultural security, loss of social status, loss of personal liberty and adult autonomy. All of these are what Speck describes as 'little deaths', and indeed the list of human experiences that involve such 'deaths' seems to be endless. Wherever there is significant change in the major circumstances affecting our daily life, there is always a degree of dying and consequently the need to grieve a little. The grief we feel for these images and reminders of our own mortality, though, is not really to be compared with the tragedy that strikes when we lose someone we dearly love, someone whom we knew as a living part of our very selves. If our life is in an intense perception of other people and things this is inevitable. By their outward gestures and inward perceptions, men and women continually strive to make sense of their environment by organising it to conform to some idea of shape and purpose that is authentically human in the sense that it is the necessary fulfilment of a basic human need. In the last chapter something was said about the unconscious foundations of this need for order and balance. The trauma of personal loss makes this need painfully apparent, so that it comes to dominate our entire consciousness. When our universe of people and things is powerfully disrupted we are lost until it has been readjusted. Sometimes, perhaps, we can 'put things right' ourselves. Characteristically, however, we need the help of other people, for our world is made up of others and draws its essential meaning from our relationship with them.

The world of the bereaved person is not only emotionally disrupted, it is cognitively shattered. He or she searches for metaphors to assimilate an experience that cannot be perceived in literal terms as the straightforward description of events but requires the language of symbolism, in which thought and feeling are united in the urgent need to be as specific as possible about matters that defy objective analysis. Events in life, stories of things that actually happened or are believed to have happened, become material for symbolic statements around which a consistent universe of discourse can be organised. During the course of my own investigations into the experience of bereavement, conducted over a period of eight years from 1971 to 1979[7] I came across some very striking examples of this:

Soon after her husband had been killed in tragic circumstances, a bereaved woman was lying in the bed they had shared when the ceiling of the room began to fall in on her. For months and even years afterwards she could think about what had befallen her only in terms of this later event. The incident provided her with a way of ordering her awareness of present and future. The ceiling became as it were the foundation for her work of reconstruction.

A man whose wife had died became ill each time her dog grew sick. When the beloved pet finally died he broke down completely for a short time. However, the death of the dog allowed him to think more clearly about his wife's death - to understand that now she really was gone - and so contributed to his recovery.

Mrs X seemed to be obsessed with the idea of cleanliness. Every time visitors called to comfort her in her bereavement she would only talk about the trouble she was having with her washing machine, a rather ancient model her husband used to repair for her from time to time. No one else seemed able to fix it: 'He was the only one who could make it work for me.' When the washing machine finally 'gave up the ghost', Mrs X took her clothes to the laundrette - and began to emerge from her own private maelstrom.

Such stories are very numerous. They show the need for clear and concise ideas that can be used to construct a kind of personal sense in situations of cognitive breakdown. They also illustrate an aspect of human grieving that has been neglected. In human affairs, ideas are not to be distinguished from the feelings they embody. We need always to make sense of our world, and this involves intellectual formulation as well as emotional acceptance, the noetic as well as the instinctual. Writers of the Freudian school, who up to now appear almost to have held the monopoly for investigations into grief and mourning, have always attributed more

importance to 'affect' than to 'cognition' because they see men and
women as motivated by instinctual drives that are fundamentally opposed
to conscious ways of perceiving the world, rather than providing the
precognitive foundation and inspiration for them. For a Freudian, conscious meanings are always suspect, because the mental processes
whereby we come to terms with our emotions are always a form of denial
of instinctual drives and of their hidden power to affect our behaviour.
Thus, the impact of loss is 'rationalised' and 'sublimated', assuming the
form of some kind of religious or philosophical explanation of human life
that is able to provide a systematic account of the disasters that befall us.
For Freud religion itself derives from the transformation of feelings caused
by the pressure of unconscious instincts. The figure of God the Father is
associated with the emergence within our awareness of the super-ego, the
force of conscience, which is a stratagem on the part of the individual ego
to divert part of the energies of the libido away from their original purpose
of instinctual satisfaction to that of self-protection and self-perpetuation:
'Thus the benevolent rule of a divine Providence allays our fears of the
dangers of life.'[8] In other words, the doctrines and ceremonies of religion
are nothing more than the by-products of what Freud calls 'the vicissitudes
of instincts' and the main purpose of the religious dramas we call rituals
is to use the symbolism of hidden and repressed states of feeling as a way
of achieving 'cathexis' - the imaginatively cued discharge of emotion
the Greeks called 'katharsis'. In other words, they simply allow us to 'let
off steam'.

There is no denying, of course, that rituals provide us with an
opportunity to express feelings that may sometimes seem out of place or
embarrassing in other situations and on other occasions. Funerals in
particular are times when we can 'get things off our chest' and share our
feelings with others. However, this is very far from being all that they do,
even from a strictly psychological point of view. The funeral is communication as well as catharsis: the transmission of ideas as well as the
ventilation of emotion. The symbolism of religious ritual embraces
infinitely more than the circumscribed needs of the individual. As Jung
makes abundantly clear, real symbolism points beyond the individual to
the other and includes within its reference the known, the unknown and the
unknowable. Symbolism is a kind of expanded thought capable of bearing
an emotional load that would otherwise remain inexpressible precisely
because it is unthinkable. The symbol enables us to come to terms on an
intuitive level with facts whose literal meaning we cannot yet deal with.
Its use is to convey a particular kind of message, one which cannot be

encoded in any other way because its significance is just too powerful for words.[9]

The relevance of this fact for human grieving is obvious. 'You have to have a funeral so that God knows you're coming,' wrote a 9-year-old girl who was asked to explain what a funeral was for. Funerals are pictures of the meaning of human death. Throughout the world, the religious mythology of cultures envisages some kind of 'journey of the dead'. Frequently this is acted out in the funeral itself. Religious belief, whether of the 'popular' or 'institutionalised' kind, demands that the journey should both be made and be seen to be made. It is a voyage from the unknown to the known; or more accurately, from what is known in experience to what is known in faith.

The performance of these symbolic dramas of departure, journey and arrival, constitutes the pledge of a spiritual transformation that is understood by those taking part in it to be compulsory. As we shall see, if the action of dismissal from the old state of being and incorporation in the new one are not carried out the person concerned is not understood to be properly dead. In culture after culture these 'unincorporated dead' are seen as inhabiting an in-between state, unable to make any progress in their journeying because of the non-performance of the appropriate action on the part of their survivors who have not 'delivered the proper message to God'. No wonder, then, that they are often so very angry and return to torment those who have cruelly and selfishly excluded them from their rightful inheritance.[10]

However absurd this may seem to a sophisticated twentieth century Western person, it may serve as a parable to illustrate a fact of our common human experience that we deny at our peril - the need for shape in human life, and particularly those aspects of it that concern us at the most vital personal level. During the spring of 1971, I carried out a limited survey of people who had lost close relatives during the past six months. Out of thirty men and women interviewed, twenty-six reported that the experience of attending the funeral had considerably relieved the distress of their loss. Half of these people told me that it was not really the things that had been said at the service that had helped, but 'just having the service'. Eight were regular churchgoers and some of these reported that the words spoken had possessed real meaning for them; however, I gained a strong impression from the survey as a whole that people felt that any service was better than no service at all. This was true even where the service was rushed and the chapel ugly and cold, or, as is so often the case, the minister a total stranger. It appears

that the compulsion to bury the dead with ceremony is strong enough
to overcome such hazards as these. It was suggested that the action of
disposing of the body in some kind of public ritual gave shape to the
dead person's life, and this itself seemed to endow the experience of the
living with a kind of significance. From a psychological point of view,
it seemed funerals were about 'rounding things off.'

All of this makes a good deal of sense, of course. For life to have
any meaning its incidents must be organised into real events, recognisable
happenings. If life does not naturally fall into convenient sections - and,
of course, it does not - then we must be able somehow to set up our own
landmarks in the flux of existence. Most of the time we do this automati-
cally: perception itself is governed by the interaction of our expectation of
recognisable sensations with our adjustment of the sensations we actually
receive into the kind of percepts that allow us to experience the world as
possessing an acceptable degree of order and harmony. Thus, contemporary psychological theory proposes the same kind of prior knowledge
about an essentially meaningful universe as is implied by Kant's 'categori-
cal imperative' and Jung's 'imago dei'. It is simply a question of who is
responsible for the final pattern, God or the individual. The relationship
that exists between the world we perceive and the one in which we live, the
world that in our search for meaning we affect and the world that affects
us, forcing us again and again to revise our picture of it, is continually being
adjusted by the mechanisms of cognition. Any major disruption of the
world about us, therefore, is a disruption of the one within us.

When this happens we cannot expect to be able to put the record
straight entirely by ourselves. At such times we need the help of other
people, not only for emotional support but also for cognitive reconstruction. These two things cannot realistically be separated, of course, and
corporate religious ritual provides us with a way of making use of their
essential coinherence in order to establish the image of personal meaning,
personal unity, in the very midst of existential chaos. The fusion of ideas
and feelings within the rite establishes it as a real event, a genuine action
undertaken to proclaim the existence of a superordinate sense in a world
other events have rendered nonsensical. By making an authoritative
statement about the final meaning of human life, and establishing that
statement as a crucial stage in a dialogue with God that continues beyond
the frontiers of the grave, funerals act to focus faith at one of the points of
greatest human need.

The Unchurched
As a new social group emerges into corporate self-consciousness so a
new 'name' is bestowed upon its members, a new belonging acknowledged by individual men and women. Expatriates, hospital patients,
prisoners, all discover this. The bereaved struggle towards it, helped on
their way by the funeral rite. Although members of expatriate communities often have some kind of religious belonging they are able to
revise and perpetuate, this does not necessarily apply to the other
groups we have been considering. Before the personal crisis occurred
which had the effect of turning them to one another and to God, many
of these acknowledged no real religious belonging at all. For reasons
that may have more to do with social structure than religious faith, they
kept their awareness of God very much to themselves. There is little
doubt that one of the causes of this state of affairs has been the
exclusiveness of what is usually called 'organised religion'. The
sociologist Thomas Luckmann[11] has claimed that when specialised
social institutions take upon themselves a monopoly of religious
authority and expertise the function of religion in 'establishing a sacred
cosmos' as a spiritual reference point for human societies may be
seriously threatened. A split tends to develop between religion and
social awareness with the result that the secular world develops its own
non-ecclesiastical sources of moral authority, while the Church and its
officers grow further and further away from the mainstream of
ordinary social life. This, says Luckmann, is what has actually happened within the Judaeo-Christian tradition, which 'represents an
extreme case of the institutional specialisation of religion'. Forced into
a defensive position by the incoming tide of social differentiation and
the ever-increasing complexity of social structures, the Christian
Church clings with growing determination to its own unique identity
as the New Israel, the Apostolic 'People of God'. Nowadays, however,
it must take its place as only one among many agencies that exist in
order to cater for the moral needs of particular groups within society.

This may be so, of course, but it is not the whole story by any
means. In some ways the polarising effect of secularisation has made the
Church more visible than it was before. Increasing social complexity, by
taking away the Church's monopoly of moral authority, has had a refining
effect upon our perception of Christianity as a specifically religious
phenomenon, rather than a convenient but rather vague way of describing
all people of good will whatever their theological beliefs or lack of them.
The men and women who approach the clergy in order to ask if they or a

member of their family may be baptised, married, buried or cremated according to the rites of the Christian Church have made a definite choice in favour of a religious ritual as opposed to any kind of civil ceremony. The fact that they come and ask, even though they admit that they do not consider themselves to be Church members in any active or practical sense, shows that they regard the Church as essentially different from other kinds of social group. Moreover they consider that a vital part of that difference is concerned with their own status as outsiders, 'strangers to the fold'. Contrary to clerical opinion it is not always social snobbery or merely a refined aesthetic sense that prompts such requests. It is often genuine religious feeling combined with an enlightened theological understanding that, in Archbishop Temple's phrase, 'the Church is the only club that exists solely for the benefit of those who are not its members'. The regularity with which they find themselves discouraged by the kind of reception that awaits them suggests that there is some disagreement about the way in which the rules of the club should be interpreted.

The confusion arises from the particular role played in the life of the Church by rites of passage. According to one view, some at least of the Church's passage rites, baptisms, marriages and funerals in particular, belong to the primal religious heritage of mankind, representing and implementing the overarching love of God for all his creation, irrespective of race, class, or religious affiliation. A main function of the Church is to make these vital services available to every man, woman and child who seeks God's blessing at those times in their lives when they have most need of it; that is, when they are setting out on a particularly important new stage of their journey through life. According to another view, however, these ceremonies are to be regarded as being vital stages in a continuing process of religious initiation. Rather than merely bringing secular life into the presence of divinity, they actually transform the nature of human life completely, so that it ceases to be 'secular' and becomes 'religious'. It seems very likely that both attitudes have always existed within the Christian Church, representing as they do complementary impulses associated with the Christian experience - the need to hold on to a personal revelation and the desire to share it with others.

Unfortunately - from the point of view of the unchurched - the Church appears to cling with increasing determination to the exclusive attitude and to be unwilling to take account of the psychological truth implicit in the other one. There is a genuine need for spiritual support at times of existential change and to ignore this fact is to run the risk of depriving the Church of the evangelistic opportunity provided by its ancient rites of passage which are, after all, intended to be the gateways into Christ's religion rather than rewards bestowed upon people who already belong to it. The Judaeo-Christian theological tradition has always held two distinct opinions about the exclusiveness of the people of God, one tending towards the idea of a salvation that is open to all comers, the other very much more exclusive, or even narrowly selective.

Christians who subscribe to the first view see the Church using the ground-swell of folk religion rather than rescuing individual survivors and establishing them in the 'safe ark of Christ's religion'. At the same time, however, a parallel school of biblical interpretation has regarded the Church as the band of specially chosen people whose destiny is to outlast the final collapse of a world that refuses to acknowledge God's law and is determined to go its own self-destructive way. In human terms, unfortunately, this tends to imply a Church that becomes more and more withdrawn and self-conscious. Something like this appears to underlie the restrictive attitudes of some churches and churchmen towards Christian initiation, whose baptismal and marital policies seem to imply that a person or family must be acceptable to the Church before they can be made acceptable to God. This scriptural tradition provides the theological rationale for the process of polarisation of society described by Luckmann, in which the Christian Church has become ever more highly organised and socially restricted.

In fact, the baptismal policies of many congregations give rise to all kinds of basic questions about what Christians really believe concerning the faith of Christ. What, exactly, is the 'good news' that the Church proclaims to all men and women? Is it that we should know enough theology, or that we should belong to the 'right' social, or even racial, grouping and have the 'right' parents and personality? Should we subscribe to an appropriate world-view, having received the correct kind of instruction, at the proper time in our lives, from teachers who are officially approved? Should we have undergone an intense psycho-spiritual experience of an approved kind? Should we in fact be already 'saved'? Should we, by our own eligibility for membership, have saved ourselves and should this eligibility consist, as it so often does, in the fact that our parents are already Church members, so that Christianity is a kind of hereditary caste? If such things are necessary in order to preserve the religious identity of the Church as the particular people of God in a secular society, who will baptise that society's longing for God?

3

The Meaning of Ritual

A theatre company presents a procession of weird beasts and birds, to celebrate someone's birthday. The poor man is dragged round by them through caverns and over streams, wet and covered in mud, bemused by it all and thoroughly happy....

In the parish church on Good Friday, priest and people lift the Sacrament from the High Altar and process to the side chapel, now a garden-tomb, where it will lie alone, surrounded by lights and flowers, until it blooms again on Easter Day....

In the Great Hall of the university the Doctor of Science trembles with terror as the time comes for her to kneel before the Chancellor. Writing the thesis was hard enough, but it was nothing compared with this! She wonders if it was worth it. And yet....

These are all rites of passage, taken at random from countless examples available throughout the world. Not all of them are overtly religious in the theological sense, but all possess a human seriousness of intention, a consciously symbolic quality. Something is happening that is too important, too true, to be simply described. If you tried to describe precisely what such things mean you would only miss the point of the argument, lose the essence of the occasion. This must be done, not talked about. It is not something about life; it is life. In this chapter we shall be looking mainly at religious ritual, but what is said here is true in principle of many of the rituals of secular life as well.

Ritual as Religious Art
In religions throughout the world, men and women use artistic form to express a well-made wish to enter God's presence. In ritual special actions and words, in some cases a particular spatial location, signify the aware-ness of the unique quality of this kind of event. The link between two

spheres of being, the divine and the human, is provided by the religious symbol, which is the conscious remembrance or actual physical representation of an historical event or an incident usually held to have taken place in a time before time, when the circumstances of mortality were definitively transcended and humanity met God face to face. Thus, art may be used within the present moment to invoke a timeless setting for encounters that take place in eternity. In this, the rite's shape is fundamental to its effect, because it is the ritual scenario that provides the 'aesthetic distance' necessary for the emotional involvement of those taking part. The rite permits a meeting of persons that under any other circumstances would be impossible. Its language, whether acted out or expressed verbally, need not be archaic, but it must, in the nature of human discourse about God, be metaphorical. Thus, for Christian believers, the name of Christ, however it may be signified, recapitulates the entire Gospel, making every act of Christian worship the actualisation of Christ's passion and resurrection.

The imagery that lies at the heart of worship is used for purposes of encounter rather than of evasion. Liturgy is a confrontation with the underlying truth of human being. It is very important to realise that the special 'world of its own' quality of the rite is to do with concentration rather than evasion. Ritual makes a special kind of point and needs a special language to do so. In the rite men and women are brought face to face with the basic issues of living and dying. We are protected in this by a mediating symbolism, but exposed to the other by the symbol's ability to induce in us an intense imaginative involvement, a revelation of identity-in-separation impelling us towards personal relationship and giving us strength for the crossing of existential thresholds. In rites of passage, the rituals by which we mark out the critical stages of our journey through life, we communicate with the divine source of our inner unity and are strengthened and refreshed for our daily lives.

The art form employed in ritual is the acted scenario, the dramatic presentation of a metaphor of personal encounter. The story of Adam and Eve, for instance, is a drama about the relationship between God and creation and illustrates the specific terms of that relationship. In many cultures throughout the world such a 'primal scenario' is given acted form wherever the intention is to refer to ultimate matters concerning the identity of the race as a whole or of its individual members. In this way the contingent events of everyday life are brought into relation with a timeless truth, an eternal, changeless reality.

The nature of art is not to inform, but to question, to say 'what is there in me for you, do you think?' At its most serious, art asks questions about the meaning and purpose of life itself, taking personal relationships for subject matter, and in drama actually using them as its medium. One could say that art asks questions about the relationship between experience and aspiration, the world as everyday reality and as ideal truth. This stands out very clearly in religious ritual, in which men and women reach out to a presence beyond themselves, but do it as themselves, in terms of their own humanity, without pretending. This is the common ground of art and religion. The struggle to give form to chaos, whether subjective or objective, a truthful shape to what was meaningless, is a continual one. The artist, like the religious man or woman, cannot stay still but continues always to search, always to aspire.

To this extent, then, religious people are artists and artists are religious. Art provides religion with the most appropriate of all languages because of its ability to communicate a message about persons in relationship without reducing it or them. Spoken and written language may faithfully transmit ideas. Only art can communicate presences. Art encourages us to regard human life as a free encounter of selves, and human perfection as the unfettered enjoyment of inter-personal love, love that can only exist in freedom. Religious ritual demonstrates this fact to perfection. The personages of the rite remain separate. They are not merged together so as to lose their unique outline, but are separate physical presences engaged in being in respect of one another. Here, in the rite, men and women draw close as they reach out for the perfection that defines and unites them. The play of relationship is acted out, its symbolism spreading outwards to include within its scope the men and women involved in the interchange of the dance, the ground where the dance takes place, the dance itself and the emblem of the dance.

Thus, in ritual, what seems to be a total dichotomy, a simple and final contradiction - God versus man, the ideal as opposed to the real - is revealed as the mystery of the unity that is between persons. In this way men and women use the imagery of art in order to express their awareness of the need for union and wholeness in situations of conflict and division, and their spiritual hunger for a way of being in which conflict and division achieve resolution. The rite makes no attempt to evade the issue. On the other hand it does not try to resolve it by argument either. Ritual demonstrates things that it admits it cannot explain, mysteries about God that cannot be explained, in terms of a mystery that is already known, the commonplace miracle of personal relationship.

One view of ritual, that of Jung, may throw some light on the kind of thing I am trying to describe. Jung sees ritual as a kind of 'acted dream', in which the conflicts between our intentions as individuals and the knowledge of God that we all share, and in which our real personhood subsists, rise to the surface, where they are acted out by real actors - the personages of the rite. 'Rituals express aptly the living process of the unconscious in the form of the drama of repentance, sacrifice and redemption.'[1]

There is certainly a very close connection between the dream conflicts described by Jung and the initiatory scenarios which characterise religious ritual throughout the world. Indeed, the place set aside outside the camp for initiations among Australian tribesmen is actually called the alcheringa, or 'dreaming place'. Ritual is by far the oldest expression of religious awareness and is found even in the most primitive cultures. In a sense the meaning and significance of all religion depends on the importance which we ascribe to it and the way we interpret it. It is 'the meaning of a truthful dream'. Consequently, to use it as a means of making precisely formulated intellectual statements is to mistake its particular nature and purpose. Certainly the message is there, but it is drawn from the rite itself by the participants rather than communicated by the rite's personages to one another or to any kind of detached 'audience'. Indeed, artistic rituals involve spectator and artist alike, making an artist out of the spectator by drawing him or her into a shared experience of discovery. This is just as much a way of clarifying experience in order to attain a uniquely personal truth as it is a method of proclaiming truths that have already been received. As in the theatre, the ritual drama requires acceptance and involvement rather than detachment: the critical intellect must wait until the curtain has fallen at the play's end.

Thus, the meaning of religious ritual is not merely something to be demonstrated by means of movement, gesture and word: it is also something to be achieved. The experience demands from us a degree of personal involvement, the gift of the self, which is painful to us. Even though our involvement in the events portrayed within the ritual drama is a vicarious one, the intention of 'giving oneself to the action' is unavoidably our own. The God who calls us to share his joy requires our first- hand appreciation of the cost involved. If we do not identify ourselves with the suffering demanded by such a transformation of essences, we can never establish within ourselves its personal meaning for ourselves and know its power to give shape to our lives. In Mircea Eliade's words 'initiation is an indispensable process in every attempt to transcend man's natural condi-

tion and attain to a sanctified mode of living'.[2] Every religious ritual is
a kind of initiation into personal truth; individuals and societies who
either ignore or are excluded from religious ritual stand in danger of
losing touch with their essential nature as beings who move forwards
in time and upward in eternity.

What I Tell You Three Times ...
The meaning of ritual may be dramatically presented by the order in which
it proceeds. This is particularly the case with those rites of passage studied
by the anthropologist van Gennep, in which the central ritual happening
is led up to, and followed by introductory and consummatory events, in
order to form a threefold complex of rites symbolising personal and
corporate change. Although it may not describe every kind of corporate
ritual, van Gennep's analysis reveals a good deal about how rites of
passage function, and repays careful attention.

Because of its tripartite shape, the rite's statement is clear, simple
and direct: for real change to take place the old situation must really end
and the new one really begin. For the new situation to 'live', the old one
must 'die'. Thus, there is always a crucial point 'between', a point
representing the condition after the old state of affairs has come to an end
and before the new one has actually begun. This is the moment of real
change, the pivotal moment that has no movement of itself, but permits
movement to take place. Thus rites give present form to future hope by
bringing home the difference between past and future, what has happened,
what is to be achieved and what the cost of that achievement will be.

One of the important things about ourselves that we customarily
forget, and of which life has to keep reminding us, is that personal change,
changes that affect us personally, take longer than we think. The fact is that
with regard to those important developments in our lives that seem to be
progressing so well, we may not have gone as far as we think. Almost
inevitably, we believe ourselves to have 'got over' emotional crises -
quarrels, disappointments, physical or psychological traumas, experiences of failure or unexpected success, whatever it may be that upsets our
expectations in a way that seriously disturbs our equilibrium - before
we actually have done. In Tom Kempinski's play Duet for One,
Stephanie, a young concert violinist who, at the very height of her
career, has contracted multiple sclerosis, vainly tries to find a way of
rebuilding her life, which has been totally disrupted by her illness. She
has no success because she has not managed to accept the fact that it
has been shattered: 'Nothing is splitting apart! Things are under

control! Everything is perfectly under control!' This is only one example, albeit a striking one, of a state of affairs well known to people who try to help those suffering from a shattered personal universe.

Many of the widows and widowers referred to me as suffering from 'pathological grieving' were in fact stuck in this world-between-worlds, whose existence they could not recognise or understand. They were reaching out for a new kind of life before they were ready to receive it, believing they could rescue themselves by an effort of will and the force of reason and only beginning to recover when they eventually had to abandon hope of any immediate deliverance and simply resign themselves to the long agony of waiting.

When we think about change we have a tendency to overlook this central period of apparent stasis. Our body knows better than we, as it adjusts in its own time to the destabilising effect of hormonal changes associated with life crises, unconvinced by the mind's assurances that nothing has really happened and that we can cope, thank you very much.

When we think and talk about change, the central factor turns out to be the crucial stage in the argument. Indeed, the effectiveness of the rite as an instrument of change may actually be that it states the importance of this central moment precisely and dramatically and so makes up for our tendency to elude the point of change. The passage rite requires us to go back to the beginning and start afresh. In it, all the circumstances of genuine existential change are symbolically portrayed, without any gloss-ing over of the central point of rest upon which real change, as distinct from mere wishful thinking, depends. An experience of progression takes the place of hopeful circumlocution. In the face of death, our own or someone else's, we indulge in this kind of psychological sleight-of-mind more readily than at any other time, ignoring the painful central stage simply because it is so painful, evading the issue in our eagerness to find reassurance and achieve stability. What we are avoiding, of course, is the factual reality of the tomb itself; we have become very skilful in convinc-ing ourselves that we have succeeded in putting all that behind us.

This is something the rite never does, however. Above all else it brings home to us the reality of our situation. It does so by similarity and by contrast. The suffering with which we identify is presented in terms of the joy that stands over against us and is also part of our truth, when this is seen in the context of a divine identity. For the community of faith, ritual's message is explicit, its demonstrations graphic. Private fantasy gives place here to public fact, which alone can stand as a basis for real change. It confronts us with the truth about life and death, demonstrating

them to us as clearly and dramatically as possible in terms of movement and gesture as well as speech. It gives a quality of concreteness
to moral decisions and movements of the soul by using the language
of place to talk about changes in time:

The passage from one social position to another is identified with a territorial
passage, such as the entrance into a village or a house, the movement from one
room to another or the crossing of streets and squares. For the semi-civilised, the
passage is actually a territorial passage.[3]

This is not simply a concept of change, a good idea about the way
things happen, but a real event in which change is known to be taking place.
What we have here is an exercise in 'lived semantics'. As such it has the
ability to counteract human denial, even the extreme defensiveness we
bring to our ideas about personal suffering and death. We are presented
with a special acted grammar of existential transformation, a way of
communicating meaning that escapes the distortions and evasions of
spoken or written language yet renders men and women eloquent by
enriching the fundamental reality of human experience of which language
is an expression. Its privileged status renders it, in a valid sense of the word,
religious. The power of this semantic difference between religious and
naturalistic truth strikes home at times of personal crisis, in the shock,
chaos and restoration of an experience vivid enough to bring about an
existential transformation.
        Such things reveal to us a universe of divine perfection that stands
over against the universe of men and things. Because they are so different
from so much of our ordinary everyday experience we need to encode
them in a symbolism that will also reveal them; a symbolism whose
dialectical nature cannot be overlooked. Somehow we must be made
aware of the violent reversal of value or significance that occurs whenever
our arrangements are brought into contact with the demand of God. The
radical nature of such happenings is very precisely signified by the
threefold shape of the rite, three being the number for revolutions, as for
perfection itself. Real change is never the simple transfer of realities, but
always a complete transformation: never a single event, always a process.
By recognising the presence of an intermediate phase we make what
happens more, not less, immediate, because it is more real, more able to
convince us of the actuality of changes as we experience them. Anybody
who has watched a character in a play stranded between past and future,
unable to move one way or the other, or who has played such a character

themselves, will recognise the true nature of this kind of threshold experience. We have all been through such things ourselves in 'real' life. It is amazing how easily we seem to forget what it was like; sometimes it needs the theatre to bring it home to us. And yet, at the very roots of our pre-conscious, our pre-perceptual experience, the watershed is basic to our being. The biochemical changes that affect our physical functioning inevitably depend on a critically important median stage that can only be described as 'neither one thing nor the other'. At whatever level of our being, it seems, we move onwards in three stages.

At the same time, and almost equally importantly, three is the number associated with climax, the climax that assists change by intensifying the conditions for its inception. The principle here seems to be the one according to which the comedian gets his audience to laugh by repeating the same catch-phrase three times. Perhaps, as some neurophysiologists have suggested, this kind of thing may be necessary for the reception and de-coding of important messages: 'Like the computing machine, the brain probably works on a variant of the famous principle expounded by Lewis Carroll in The Hunting of the Snark - "what I tell you three times is true".[4] Certainly, the threefold order implies authority, definiteness and optimism, the optimism expressed in such phrases as 'third time lucky', or, as Shakespeare has it, 'the third time pays for all'. But the rite's triplicity is also three-dimensional, for here, as in the theatre, communication takes place in depth. The characters are people and not merely ideas. They communicate within the given circumstances of human relationship and not in any abstract context. Thus, to the qualities of authority, optimism and definition of action we must add notions of solidity and practicality. The rite is not simply a good idea, it is a usable experience, too.

In fact, the thing that brings reality and meaning into a succession of events is precisely this element of recognisable shape, without which nothing really makes any sense at all to us. A basic purpose of rituals is the effective proclamation of the possibility of shape in human experience. So many of our experiences as human beings make the achievement of significant form critically necessary to us. In such situations the human mind finds it almost impossibly hard to restore integrity to its perception of the universe, and must somehow be helped to do so. An intervention both salutary and heroic is called for: an infusion of meaning and shape that will allow it at least a possibility of unity. The rite of passage aims to contain men and women in a three-dimensional mise-en-scène of ideal relationships, to convince them with a threefold assurance of purpose and hope and to establish them in the new life of the future. To contain, but not to constrain, for the rite's action is one of liberation not restriction, and its symbolism one of ultimate meaning perceived as an endless source of truth. The idea of a contained openness is fundamental to ritual, where the element of shape contributes to freedom in a way that eludes its two-dimensional expression within the mandala. The rite contains the static and the dynamic, the image of a changeless perfection and the revelation of truth-as-movement, purpose, growth, able to move heart as well as head because it is so like life itself.

To conclude this chapter, then: the rite has an effect on the human awareness that is uniquely integrative. It works by both event and argument, making use of the right hemisphere of the brain - the figurative, intuitive, creative side, which has 'an important role in the expression and appreciation of emotion'[5] - and marrying its characteristic mode of construing reality to ideas of life and death that fall within the scope of the left brain - the hemisphere that examines, compares and concludes. At its most effective, the rite is not only a powerful argument, it is a convincing experience.

4

Rites of Passage and Initiation:
Baptisms, Marriages and Funerals

In his seminal book on rites of passage, the Dutch anthropologist, Arnold van Gennep, described how, from time immemorial, men and women have found ritual an essential tool for living:

For groups as well as individuals, life itself means to separate and to be re-united, to change form and condition, to die and be reborn. It is to act and to cease, to wait and rest and then to begin acting again, but in a different way.[1]

We have seen how passage rites attempt to deal creatively with change as an unavoidable fact of human life. The individual member of society is involved in a whole succession of public ceremonies that are vital to him or her personally, and that act as a special kind of doorway into a new stage of life.

In corporate ritual, a religious doctrine concerning the emergence of life out of death is presented to us in a particular way, so that change in the nature and quality of our own personal reality is perceived as a real event, something taking place in the structure of life itself rather than just an idea or an abstract concept. On the one hand the use of real 'actors' helps to bring home the situation of men and women who are living through crucial changes in their individual experience and social and religious status. On the other hand, the way in which the rite is constructed, and in particular the way in which its constituent parts follow one another, is of the greatest importance with regard to its practical function as a model of transformations taking place at the deepest psychological level of personal identity.

Van Gennep points out that 'a complete scheme of rites of passage includes pre-liminal rites (rites of separation), liminal rites (rites of transition) and post-liminal rites (rites of incorporation)'.[2] Because of its overall shape the three movements of the rite are mutually suggestive, each referring to, and in a sense including, both of the others. The reversal of our ordinary ways of doing things, of everything we are used to and have come to expect signals the onset of chaos before it can be resolved into a new universe of freedom and love. At some stage in its organisation every rite must inform us clearly and unmistakably that 'the time is out of joint'. There must be wrongness and outrage, so that what is presented to us for our participation is an authentic image of what has become the true state of affairs for us - a world no longer recognisable, from which all rightness has been obliterated by a happening of monumental wrongness. In rituals throughout the world this sense of outrage, which signifies the awareness of a radical discontinuity, the overturning and disruption of arrangements and attitudes belonging to the ordinary experience of living, is reproduced in all its savage intensity as the vital step towards its eventual resolution. But this is not the whole story, of course. Nor is it the crucial part. Self expression, however dramatically explicit, will not save us from the turmoil we find ourselves in; we must have help to survive. Having discovered the reality of our situation we call out to a source of life outside ourselves, someone who both knows our condition and is able to rescue us from it. The rite of passage is a journey towards the divine source of being which is undertaken in partnership with a person who is able to guide us where we need to go, if we are to survive. To answer our need he must not merely summon us from far away, because we are not able to cope alone. Instead, he must actually journey alongside us to our destination. He must be a divine traveller, able to suffer and triumph in our company.

This vital understanding is embodied in a ritual drama having as its protagonist a person or group who embrace within their destiny two distinct realities, human and divine. The rite recognises that these realities are irreconcilable, and that at some point the hero-saviour must abandon his mortal nature. Even here the rite of passage preserves the honesty of its picture of a true meeting between man and God; for the action whereby the rite's central figure proclaims his divinity is the most characteristically human action of all, that of consciously experiencing his own death.

Participation in the ritual scenario has the effect of accustoming us to the idea of our own death, now to be seen in the special resurrection context presented by the rite. It is Christ's presence in the rite, however, that brings the idea home to us - we are helped to live with our fear of dying through a personal relationship with the one who has conquered death. Our new courage is gracious rather than natural, and our new identity partakes of divinity. As Clem Gorman says, ritual leads us 'into higher ground'.[3] It is a responsive action undertaken in obedience to God's own call, not something that we ourselves simply decide to embark upon. In the original happening symbolised by the rite, God's message is proclaimed in a way that is both unmistakable and unforgettable. The message is about change - the need for it and the means whereby it is attained. It is the most vital message of all. As Mircea Eliade says, 'initiation and its patterns are indissoluble with the very structure of spiritual life'.[4]

It is gift as well as message - or rather, gift as message - delivered in the language of a transformed humanity, one that has been summoned to triumph over every kind of death in the name of the Lord of Life. To put this in another way, the rite is a responsive imitation of his original saving action, one in which we address him in the language he himself uses to make himself personally known to his world: the language of death and resurrection, the saving action of the Word made flesh.

In the remaining part of this chapter we shall be looking at the three most important 'transformations' that are still given ritual expression in modern Western society in the form of rites of passage of varying degrees of adequacy - baptisms, marriages and funerals. To do this we shall move away slightly from anthropological observation and take a more theological position, as we consider how Christian belief and experience affects the way we organise our rituals of transition. What is the relationship between Christian baptism, marriage and disposal of the dead and the kind of rites of passage we have been considering? From the point of view of individual rites, the first two are still close to their original form. Alone, the treatment of death has suffered mutilation at the hands of social convenience.[5] In the next chapter the theme is continued, as we look briefly at the sacraments in their identity as rites of passage for the Christian Church.

BAPTISM
Baptism and Personal Names
Baptism is the Christian rite of passage par excellence. Its meaning is fully personal and yet entirely corporate as it embodies the doctrine of membership of the Body of Christ. Christian baptism, our initiation into the dying and rising of Christ, is the concern of the entire race; the sin baptism exists to counter is human sin at its most widespread and least individual. However its cosmic nature does not make it any the less personal. The inheritance of all, it must be taken account of by each ('Taken account

of' - what a universe of implication in the innocent sounding phrase!)
It is this inherited sinfulness that makes us feel most helpless. Not only
my own feelings but every other Christian's too. As St Paul says 'who
shall deliver me from the body of this death?'

The idea of inherited sin, of a tendency towards disobedience
that has become part of human nature itself, accords with the practice
of infant baptism. A baby's sin must be 'original' if he or she needs to
be baptised at all - and to this extent the practice of baptising infants
is justified by the dramatically explicit way in which this fundamental
theological point is brought home. There can be no other reason for
taking the most innocent people we can find and making a public
ceremony of washing their sins away. As those of us who are priests
never stop having to explain to the parents of the babies we baptise, we
need holy baptism in order to atone for something we cannot help,
which we have whether we want it or not, and which, apart from the
sacramental grace of Christ, we cannot possibly be rid of. It does not
matter whether we understand it, we have it - or rather it has us.

This sounds impersonal, and of course it is. Sin is always destructive of personality, and original sin is the most anti-personal kind
of all. Or almost the most anti-personal. In fact, the Bible sees a more
powerfully destructive force at work in the world than even original
sin. Throughout the Old and New Testaments, the figure of Satan is
shown undermining the relationship that exists between man and God,
and man and man. In corrupting the relationship between persons,
Satan destroys the life of entire communities. Indeed it is because of his
influence over the whole human race that so many of Jesus's healing
miracles are presented as individual exorcisms. The sufferings that
afflict men and women are not intended to be seen as the result of
individual sinfulness, but of that proneness to every kind of corruption,
physical, mental and spiritual, that is Satan's gift to the human race as
a whole. It is to free mankind from this tyranny that the Word became
flesh.

The attribution of personhood to Satan is misleading; we are
talking of an anti-personal impulse, a negative force undermining human
personality, potentially destroying the authentic being of man and woman
by turning them against the source of life itself. Whereas original sin is a
kind of passivity, a proneness to evil, Satan is the active power of evil
itself. Although this works in and through human nature it does not
originate in it, but simply makes use of it in warfare against God. The Bible
makes it clear that this campaign cannot succeed; indeed its failure was

assured before the beginning of time itself, and since Christ's victory on the cross, men and women have been in possession of the truth that is able to set them free from the power of evil to control their lives and prevent them from attaining to the full perfection of personhood, 'a perfect man, the measure of the stature of the fulness of Christ'.[6]

Such is the view of Satanic evil that St Paul expresses so very forcibly in his epistles, particularly Ephesians and Colossians: 'For our fight is not against human foes, but against cosmic powers, against the authorities and potentates of this dark world, against the superhuman forces of evil in the heavens'.[7] Superhuman, and yet, in a sense, subhuman, because sub-personal. The relationship that binds men and women together at a personal level is set within the hostile and destructive context of a cosmic principle that is anti-relationship, human society being the arena in which the battle for personhood is fought out. It is not human society itself that is evil, but what, under the influence of Satan, we have made of it by using it in ways that are destructive of relationship and expressive of our alienation from God and one another. What St Paul is describing here is the phenomenon which Charles Masson calls 'L'action impersonelle du siècle'.[8] Paul's way of putting it is rather more dramatic however. As we saw earlier, the figure that dominates the entire action, directing the warfare against the sons and daughters of God, is the most terrifying spectre of all, the very negation of any human meaning, so anti-human as not even to merit a name.

It would be impossible to overestimate the importance of this. Having a personal name is the pre-requisite of being considered - and of considering oneself - to be fully human. Machines, computers, robots, have numbers or identification codes. Only the subjects and objects of human regard, human love, have names. To give a person a name is to endow him or her with the humanity needed for living among people. Indeed, to give any kind of living creature a name is to bestow personality upon it. Other animals can live without a personal name though: we cannot. Psychologically speaking, our name is our most treasured possession, the certificate of our membership of human society, our passport to the country inhabited by the rest of the human race. It is the way in which we are recognised and acknowledged by other people as ourselves, and the token of our willingness to take account of our duties and responsibilities towards the others with whom we live. It is the key word in the language of social belonging and consequently of our personal identity.

In communities where the sense of corporate identity is strong, and the 'nomos' of society well established, an individual's name is more precious than ever, precisely because it represents a particular position within a closely-knit network of names, and consequently of duties, so that to deny a name is literally to refuse to acknowledge a place in society. In situations where human existence is considered to be directly congruous with social belonging - for example in some of the tribal societies described by anthropologists - the ritualised removal of a name is received by the unfortunate victim as a sentence of death; indeed, it may actually have the effect of killing him. In the same way, to give a name is to give life, because it is to put someone in the right way of living in society with others by making them accountable to God and man, for as St Thomas says 'it is specifically the same act whereby we love God and whereby we love our neighbours'. To name is to transform; to strengthen the vulnerable and encourage the fainthearted; to locate those who are displaced, or as yet unplaced, or who stand in danger of losing their way in the terrifying new world that lies before them.

In rites of passage the purpose of naming, locating, strengthening, is made explicit, and certain techniques are used to give it social (and consequently personal) reality. As we saw in Chapter 1 other names are not necessarily cancelled out; where they are retained the significance of the rite is to establish them more firmly. It is identity that is asserted and established, not a label. Even where no name is formally bestowed the person's identity is changed. Transformation is not seen as an idea but as a tangible experience. It is not preached about and meditated upon, it is something done, and done publicly - something to be seen and heard, suffered and savoured. Like a play or a symphony, the rite of passage is a genuine public event, with power to affect the way in which people organise their lives together. As we have seen, throughout the world the experience of spiritual renewal by means of an existential transformation is made actual by movement, gesture, music, dancing and singing - in other words, by expressive action and symbolic structure. Because the transformation that is celebrated and realised here is one concerning the relationship of persons - a metamorphosis of everything that takes place between and among them - the approach is not solely or even primarily through ideas but images. A living iconography that makes extensive use of the whole range of human expressiveness; a truly incarnational way of communicating truths that concern human life in its fullness and complexity.

Simply by listening to people who have recently been present at a service for infant baptism, it is possible to reach a good idea of what actually took place, particularly the part where the priest or minister took the baby in his arms, held him over the font and sprinkled water over him 'in the name of the Father, the Son and the Holy Spirit', the threefold action giving dramatic emphasis to the simple ceremony. What you will hear about from the people actually present is not what was said on the occasion, but what was done, including, most probably, some vivid details about the baby's own contribution to the proceedings. Baptism is definitely a 'doing'. (Strangely enough, in adult baptism, which is rapidly becoming the norm in many parts of the world, the effect can be even more striking. In such a setting grown men and women appear more vulnerable than babies.)

Theologically sophisticated people may look askance at the 'crudity' of all this - but it certainly makes its point. The symbolism is powerful, far more so than the explanation that accompanies the actions at the font, which itself has to be explained before it can throw any light on the particular situation of this child and these parents. The 'natural symbolism' of water as source of life and agent of profound change, archetype of primal security and existential danger - the 'sea changes' that affect human experience in ways we find impossible to contemplate - the ceremonial taking, washing, and handing over to the representatives of the congregation - involve the imagination at a level that requires that consideration of their true significance must wait until the ceremony is over and those involved have returned to their own place and time in order to continue their daily lives. As in all drama, whether it be human or divine, understanding waits upon encounter rather than the other way round. If we analyse something too much while we are actually involved in the performance of it, we run the risk of forfeiting the enlightenment we seek. Enlightenment has a way of arriving at its own speed, not ours.

This is not to say that an intellectual grasp of Christian doctrine about baptism is not important: but that its real meaning and significance tend to occur to us subliminally and are registered retrospectively. Our Lord himself takes account of this fact, distracting our attention from ourselves by telling us stories about other people, and from himself by coming to meet us in the ordinary harmless things of life, water, bread and wine. The impact of the symbolism of infant baptism is aimed at the child's parents and godparents, and quite literally goes over the head of the actual candidate!

Certainly, the parents of children brought into church should listen to the minister and try to attend to the instruction given during the service about the meaning of Christian baptism. However, they should not be too discouraged if the theory behind what is happening seems a little unreal to them. The fact is that acceptance of the personal relevance of baptism comes only from commitment to Christ, which itself comes from experience - experience of the transforming power of the Holy Spirit. What happened at the service, the actual event at which we were present and in which we ourselves took part, is crucial to our understanding of our own vocation when our own ears and eyes are opened and we are able to see the Lord under the forms of Christian doctrine.

This certainly casts doubt on the reasonableness of the widespread practice that demands a high degree of personal commitment to the Christian faith on the part of the parents as a prerequisite for baptism of the child. What is suggested instead is that what actually happens is not that we eventually come to learn the true meaning of the sacrament when we have been duly instructed in the ideological significance of the scriptures, but that the rite itself, although strange and mysterious at the time, is the crucial experience which, when the time comes, brings its own kind of understanding to the doctrine. We have to proceed in faith, waiting for the drama to unfold itself. This is something that cannot be forced, and we should not try to force it either upon ourselves or other people. No one should demand intellectual assent as the price of involvement in mystery. The first thing we must be willing to do for any rite of passage - and particularly infant baptism - is to let it speak for itself!

The Shape of Baptism

In its original place at the Vigil of Easter, the turning point of the Christian year, baptism was the fulcrum of a sequence of ceremonies effecting the renewal of the whole creation, as it brought the divine life to more and more men and women within the world. With each new batch of candidates time itself, the emerging year, was baptised. The shape of the primitive Easter cycle seems to have been as follows:

LENT   Preparation, involving separation from the world

leading to:

HOLY WEEK The time of testing, culminating in the baptism
              on Easter Eve, the symbolic analogue of the
              events of Good Friday and Holy Saturday

culminating in:

EASTER TO The emergence of the new Church, the Easter People
PENTECOST

     Historically, the shape of baptism as a ternary complex of ceremonies emerges quite early on, although the New Testament picture is not very clear and does not warrant the claim that a threefold ritual can be distinguished. There are descriptions of, and references to, the baptismal event, but its association with other rituals such as the laying on of hands is by no means definite and cannot be taken as constituting a general pattern for initiation. By the third century A.D., the procedure has become more complex. As described by Hippolytus and Tertullian, baptism starts with a whole series of actions of a pre-liminal kind, including instruction of catechumens, blessing of water, threefold renunciation of the devil by the candidates. In the baptism itself the procedure was also threefold, as three professions of faith accompanied three immersions. Anointing, episcopal blessing and a 'first meal' of honey and milk for the newly reborn made up the post-liminal rite.[9] Obviously, the emergence in popularity of the practice of baptising infants made these extensive procedures impracticable; however, the order of the rite was maintained during the years to come.[10]

     The pattern stands out clearly today; more clearly, perhaps, in the Roman Catholic tradition than the Protestant, possibly because of the latter's strong leanings towards verbal instruction. Modern Anglicanism has returned to a more primitive form of passage rite, aiming at clarity of structure as well as conciseness of speech. Certainly the use of ordinary speech instead of Latin or seventeenth-century English has made the event more immediate and allowed its shape to speak more eloquently. The Roman Catholic Rite of Baptism for Children (1969) is divided into five parts, the first three of which fall naturally into the shape of a pre-liminal rite (Reception of the Child, Celebration of God's Word, Exorcism Prayer). In this section the child is formally separated from the society of his or her family in preparation for entry into the special privileged world of those who have 'put on Christ'. The meaning of what is about to happen is made clear to all present as the personal name to be borne by the future member of Christ's Body is announced and parents and godparents are examined as to their particular responsibilities. All present are reminded as to the nature of their Christian calling by means of a reading (or readings) from the gospels and a short address. All of this constitutes the Church's declaration of intent with regard to this particular child: 'Look lovingly on this child who is to be baptised.' As the final stage in this first section the initiand is symbolically prepared, in body and soul, by actions of anointing and exorcism, which signify deliverance from spiritual (and consequently physical) bondage. He or she is ready to receive the Spirit.

The actual baptism takes place after the preparatory separation, parents and godparents responding in the person of someone too young to 'speak up' for themselves. This is the crucial threshold phase of the rite of passage, and it brings home membership of Christ's body with particular force in infant baptism, as child, parents and godparents together symbolise elements of emergent life as they portray the interdependence of the family and the dependence of all on Christ. This is portrayed by the actions of clothing and the reception of a lighted candle, bringing the liminal rite to an end.

To conclude the baptismal liturgy, the congregation sing a hymn and give thanks to God in a procession, prayers and the recitation of the Lord's Prayer. This is followed by the Blessing.

The same shape is preserved in the Anglican Service of Infant Baptism, in the Alternative Service Book. The first part of the service - the Duties of Parents and Godparents, the Ministry of the Word - sets the scene for the baptism. In it parents and godparents undertake to give the child 'the help and encouragement (he or she) needs ... to be faithful in public worship and prayer, to live by trust in God, and come to confirmation ... by your prayers, by your example and by your teaching'. A homily is provided, and/or an appropriate gospel passage suggested. Finally this part of the rite is summed up in a petition, made by all present, that this child may be received into 'the family of the Church'. The decision and baptism constitute the heart of the rite. At this decisive, midway point, parents and godparents, speaking for themselves and the child, make their promises to 'turn to Christ', 'repent of their sins' and 'renounce evil': the child is baptised and signed with the cross; affirmations of belief and trust in the Holy Trinity are made by parents and godparents. The rite of passage signifies the new condition that has been achieved by shaping its final movement into a corporate gesture of welcome, as the body of Christ is enriched by the presence of a new member. Thanksgiving prayers are said, culminating in the Lord's Prayer.

For many Christians, of course, only the Eucharist can truly consummate the kind of existential change envisaged in such a rite of passage; which is why many congregations perform the baptismal rite during Mass. It is at least questionable as to whether this does not to some extent lessen the sacramental significance of a rite of passage specifically designed to stand on its own. First and foremost the theme of baptism is that of solitariness. It is about separation. The two services of baptism described here present a change in the social identity of an individual that is total and irreversible, starting and ending with public pronouncements about identity-as-belonging, the terms of which will be, or have been, wholly changed, and centring upon an experience that is itself completely individual. In this case the central image is of a unique agony and deliverance, the personal application of a corporate experience. In the rite's crucial phase it focusses upon the initiand, who cannot even pronounce the words he or she needs in order to make the vital saving response, but must accept life from others and be joined to the community of faith in order to survive as a living soul. At this central point in the baptism service, godparents and parents devote their being entirely to the child, surrendering their own identity to this potential member of Christ's body as the means whereby he or she may gain membership.

Thus the Church makes its meaning clear in its own special way through its sacramental rituals, acting out what is too profound to be expressed in any other way. Unity and individuality, the divine nature of personhood that abides in the self that is perpetually lost and found in the other, is presented to us in infant baptism in terms of the soul's journey from an undifferentiated union of natural belonging to the loving fellowship of redeemed creatures. This is a journey via the loneliness of a crucial individual transformation, presented not simply as an idea to be entertained, but as an experience that has been lived through. On the part of those who have undertaken responsibility for the child's spiritual welfare the reflections to which this rite has given rise may last a lifetime.

MARRIAGE
Marriage and Immortality

First of all some words about the actual process of getting married. If baptism symbolises setting forth on the journey, marriage is the rite of passage that epitomises voyaging. Marriage speaks to us of the conditions of our life in media res. This is because it is the sacrament of human relationship at its closest and most fundamental, the sacrament of 'lived life'. As we have seen, in every rite of passage, an eternal truth is expressed in terms of its embodiment in the way we experience life in a changing world. To put this in another way, the function of the symbol in bridging the vertical gap between the state of affairs in human society and its counterpart in the ideal society of the kingdom of heaven is extended horizontally into time and space. This happens in order to express the idea, and reproduce the experience, of a process of change or development taking place over a period of time within the course of human life. Contrasting conditions of life, positions accepted within society both human and divine, experiences of human relationship, views of the meaning and purpose of human existence, are here placed in succession, arranged about a central period of transformation. The symbolism of the meeting between God and man is expressed in terms of 'before', 'during' and 'after', rather than 'higher' and 'lower'. In this practical form the initiatory symbol can be acted out in public by the people whom the rite concerns and the transformation be worked through. Thus, ideas of separation and union, key concepts for any understanding of marriage are embodied in a ritual that takes as its symbol an actual journey to a real destination and uses this to signify both a spiritual journey into the being of love, and a temporal voyage, a passage through time, undertaken within a human relationship that will grow ever deeper and more real as it is conformed to the spiritual pilgrimage with which it is homologised. Two kinds of initiation are envisaged here - the divinisation of the soul through a human love that is the living symbol of the divine one ('Christ's love for his Church') and the carrying on of biological life from one individual lifetime to the next by the natural process of procreation, the succession of events according to which we are born, give birth ourselves and die.

This 'cultural immortality', as it is sometimes called, may also be regarded as a way of defeating death; indeed it is frequently seen as such by people who do not believe in any kind of personal immortality. Even for these, then, the marriage service is an initiation into a kind of life that transcends the limits set by the lifetime of individual men and women.

This too is, in a sense, a genuinely religious intention; for it is quite plainly stated in the marriage service that 'marriage is given that [the married couple] may have children and be blessed in caring for them and bringing them up in accordance with God's will, to his praise and glory' (ASB). Married people, then, are supposed to have children, if they can, not simply in order to perpetuate the race so as to carry out purely human purposes, but also, in a very real way, to implement God's own will. By giving birth to children in a spirit of obedience and love, we are conformed to God's being by participating in his divine creativity. However, the new human lives that result from this are able to serve God not simply by being born and in the fullness of time going on to give birth themselves, but by taking a full, active part in the creative process of helping to build God's kingdom among men and women. As Stanley Hauerwas expresses it:

Nothing is so important as the having and rearing of children ... not because we assume that our children will somehow be better than we are, but because we hope our children will choose to be the next generation of those that carry the glory of God in the world.[11]

The Function of Display

As with baptisms, so with weddings. Clergy often accuse people of wanting to be married in church for the wrong reasons, by which they mean that the impulse is not related to a specifically Christian commitment; it has more to do with feelings than with the will and is more sentimental than rational. It concerns a desire for display rather than the need to make a solemn promise to God. Even more than in the case of baptism, there appears to be a good deal of 'romantic nonsense' surrounding these events.

From the point of view we are taking here, however, which is to look at marriage specifically as a rite of passage, this may be to confuse the issue somewhat. In weddings, as well as baptisms, this 'nonsense' is very important. It is all part of the business of setting the scene for a particular kind of event that cannot really be said to take place at all unless the scene is set for it. To be solemn, to have a serious intention, is not the same thing as to be sober and restrained or dull and prosaic (although we in England may frequently confuse the two attitudes). Indeed, both words have two meanings, one concerned with mood and the other with a disposition of heart and mind. A festive mood may contribute to an occasion that is literally 'unforgettable', a part of life 'set apart' by an intense concentration of experience, a focussing of thought and action, a purposeful combination of artistic skill and organisational effort to produce the occasion of something of quite special importance. One way or another this kind of occasion possesses an unavoidably religious significance, because it is in this way that as men and women we register our transcendent intentions. We give expression to ideas and purposes that are quite beyond the scope of the things we usually say and do, because they concern a disposition of the self, of the entire person, that we would otherwise have difficulty in finding words for. At this level we acknowledge the divine even while (somewhat desperately it sometimes seems) clinging to an 'honest' theological scepticism.

Standing outside the situation, disturbed by what seems to be a deplorable lack of spiritual awareness on the part of those involved, we may be distracted by all the fuss, seeing it, as dispassionate spectators often regard funerals, as simply a way of displaying wealth and attracting attention to social prestige, which it may partly be, of course. There is a serious purpose for the display though, and a valid reason for the expense: 'We made a real splash of it. After all, it only happens once in their lives, doesn't it?' Weddings, like baptisms and funerals, may be public events, but they certainly reveal a very clear and definite division between 'insiders' and 'outsiders'. You either come along and are to some degree initiated into the proceedings or you stand on the other side of the street, preserving your right to observe and comment on whatever is going on. You certainly cannot do both.

In fact, of course, all those familiar wedding associations that cause so much discomfort to sensible, sober-minded people - ideas of Hollywood romance, adolescent yearnings, commercialised hoo-ha, romantic nonsense - have meaning and significance within the ritual context. They are all part of the way in which human beings react when they find themselves in the presence of things that are really important. On such occasions, for reasons directly connected with human vulnerability, people often become less rather than more serious. Rites of passage are specially constructed in order to take this fact into account and put it to good use in the service of a sincere and solemn intention. This frivolity is part of the candour about the human condition that the ritual process offers to God, receiving in exchange, as it were, a strength of purpose that comes from the experience of sharing in his divine being. The connection between an element of display and a fundamentally serious purpose is of course familiar to students of animal behaviour. Many species of animals, birds and insects communicate by 'acting out' their intentions in ritualised displays of behaviour that is not, in fact, what it appears to be. By making a show of aggression or friendliness, it is possible to transmit a powerfully

explicit message about the possibility of 'real' - that is directly instru-
mental - behaviour taking place in the future. Because its purpose is to
present meaning rather than to carry out executive action, such display
behaviour tends to be rather exaggerated; after all, its main purpose lies in
its pictorial value. It is often concerned with the avoidance of conflict and
the desire to form new alliances. Indeed it is specifically associated with
mating.

As long as human beings have existed, weddings have been
occasions for the formation of new social groupings. Not only do they
represent the extension of relationships between families, which may or
may not have previously been socially accepted, they are also occasions
when long-standing rivalries within families are abandoned and traditional enmities laid to rest. This, again, is something envisaged by the
ritual process. As we have seen, the rite presents us with the symbolic
resolution of the greatest, most radical opposition of all, that between the
human and the divine: in this context, ordinary human differences, even
long-standing jealousies and resentments are temporarily suspended, and
sometimes permanently healed.

Ever since Durkheim, anthropologists have drawn attention to the
action of ritual in implementing the harmony to which it aspires. Max
Gluckman in particular stresses the rite's reconciling nature, its ability to
harmonise the discord between present social or interpersonal reality and
the wholeness and unity of the religious idea. Attitudes that exist in painful
opposition to the social status quo are brought into alignment by the ritual
process as conflicts are acted out and resolved within the sacred milieu.
Similarly, Victor Turner has investigated corporate rituals of social
change in so-called 'primitive' societies. His description of rites of
passage underlines the resolution of discord at the personal level -
'among themselves, [those passing through the ritual process] tend to
develop an intense comradeship and egalitarianism. "Secular" distinc-
tions of rank and status disappear or are homogenised.'[12]

As we saw in Chapter 1, a study of the actual working of religious
ritual reveals that the rite is always concerned to hold opposing forces in
tension. It brings together the world of contingent reality and that of
ultimate truth in a creative way, not by merging the two together, but by
allowing them to encounter each other, so that the world of men and
women is refreshed and renewed by contact with the ideal society of divine
reality. Indeed, the ceremonial proclamation of reconciliation obviously
implies the fact that oppositions exist in the situation to which it refers; and
every rite of passage transmits clear images of chaos and confusion, the

symbolic analogues of the human problems it exists in order to resolve. This is obviously relevant to the difficulties involved in forming alliances between families; as we shall see, it is even more striking in connection with the state of affairs concerning funerals and human grieving. The heart of the matter is that in order to be authentic, the rite must always contain chaos, if only because, in the presence of divine order and perfection, chaos is revealed as simple human truth. For relationship to be achieved, truthfulness must be preserved.

Marriage and the Relationship of Individuals

Perhaps most importantly of all, at least from the point of view of our understanding of passage rites, the ritual of marriage expresses and allows a kind of relationship between people that even in this life allows them a measure of divinity because it is, genuinely and realistically, a sharing in the true nature of love and, to this extent, a way of participating in the Being of God himself. This is the real meaning of the service. These values of human living are worked out in other ways apart from within the bond of marriage, of course, but in a real sense marriage represents all close personal relationships in which we are bound by mutual love and give life to and receive life from one another - which is why I have called it the sacrament of 'lived life'.

Just as baptism is basically concerned with the naming of individuals - and so has vital implications for our sense of personal identity, what psychologists refer to as our self-image - so marriage is about our immediate personal relationships, the need to give oneself to another person and receive oneself back from them in the interchange of human love. You might say, indeed, that marriage is the most extreme case of human relationship. It establishes the union of two individuals in as complete and final a way as is humanly possible, and asks God to make up the deficiencies of human intention and human capability by bestowing all the riches of his grace upon the relationship between them. Consequently it serves as a test case for other loving relationships; a man and a woman who embrace its true meaning may develop, and grow into, an understanding of what a human relationship really is that will affect their outlook on life itself.

Paradoxically, in the intimacy of marriage the essential separateness and individuality of human personhood, the loneliness of being human, is presented very forcibly. The most striking thing about a happily married couple is the way that each brings out the other's individuality, as each enjoys the things about the other that are different from him or her self. This, after all, is why they fell in love, and in a happy marriage it remains the most precious thing about the relationship. Whatever is shared is a new creation, owing part of its existence to each partner, but never really belonging to either in the sense of being a part of their individuality. The individuality persists, as the source of what is common. In fact, it increases. The children of a happy marriage are the living proof of the soundness of this principle as they reflect the love between their parents in ways that are entirely individual to themselves. It has been said that the members of a happy family are like a group of trees growing together on the top of a hill: they share the same soil, are refreshed by the same rain and nourished by the same sunlight, but they do not grow in one another's shadow.[13]

It is a fact that the more we learn of relationship the more we discover about God, for the Holy Trinity is itself, of course, just such a relationship. Indeed, it is the original and final relationship of people in love, the spiritual reality, of which every genuine human relationship is the sacramental symbol. Just as, theologically speaking, God, the being of love, is a relationship of three persons, so also our human experience of love is threefold. That is to say, not only can we imagine a scheme or model of the being of love that is in three parts, aspects or movements, the existence of any one of which necessarily involves the presence of the other two (as, for instance, original or fundamental love, active or creative love, unitive or responsive love, or love as something given, received, and returned), but we actually have an experience of loving that in its completeness is itself threefold, as it is not to be separated from the experience of being loved and the experience of desiring the other to enjoy the love that we ourselves are receiving. There is an interchange of loving regard that does not originate in either subject, but gives life to both, so that we can truly say that the creative presence in our experience of love is neither in us nor outside us, but between us.

The unity of love is in relationship rather than through synthesis. It is a unity that must depend on freedom, in the possibility of independence. By demonstrating the physical reality of men and women, by defining them as separate individuals, ritual draws attention to the invisible presence that lives between them, the mutuality of relationship that at once unites them and preserves their independent selfhood. The structure of the rite, by presenting the words, movements and gestures by which they act towards one another, distinguishes and defines the relationship that lives among them, revealing it as the source of their unique personal life, as distinct from their biological existence. At the same time, however, the latter is seen to be the essential prerequisite of all such relationships, for there is no gift of the self that would hold the body back from service of the other, and it is the body that makes the ritual gestures and carries out the ritual movements. The body is the pledge and emblem of the individual self's outgoing love, for it is this physical presence that is given away in love and service to the other, to be received back again in the other's own embodied action towards the self.

'With my body I thee worship.' The pledge given and received and the gesture that accompanies it, whereby each takes the hand of the other, expresses the heart of the marriage service. Christian marriage is the sacrament of human incarnateness: of the fusion of body and spirit that is the individual, private self, and of the free encounter of selves that makes us into people. It is wholly appropriate that what could be regarded as primarily a legal contract should be given ritual form, so that the separate identity of each of the partners is clearly presented and their movement towards each other, their joyous acceptance of the other as the other, is the mode of their self-offering to God. With its explicit reference to mutual forbearance and reciprocal love, Christian marriage is the sacrament of redeemed human personality, the single self that gives itself wholly away in love. The gift can only be bestowed in and through Christ, for only the Redeemer can surrender and receive himself in this way.

The Shape of Marriage
The true identity of marriage as a post-liminal, unitive, ritual stands out very clearly when it takes its place within the extended ritual complex described by van Gennep. In many less developed cultures throughout the world, the actual marriage ceremony is preceded by well-defined rites of separation and transition. The initiatory significance of the ritual process is clearly distinguished from its unitive force by the stress laid on the pre-liminal and liminal movements of the rite. In many cultures the pre-liminal stage consists of a ceremonial agreement between the two families involved in the proposed marriage, something that no longer takes place in our own society. The liminal period is the time of betrothal. This is characterised by the kind of ritual practices that are typically associated with the moment of crucial change itself, in other words they involve the reversal of the normal style of life of the girl or boy receiving initiation. Sometimes this transitional phase involves sexual initiation, sometimes it takes the form of a period of strict seclusion in preparation for emergence into new life as a married person, involving confinement in a symbolic 'womb', which is also, and equally importantly, the tomb in which the old

life is laid to rest. It is always a time of chaos, however, calling to mind the tradition that survived in Christian Europe for many centuries, according to which the couple involved in the process of becoming married were ceremonially put to bed together amid scenes of great hilarity. The marriage ceremony proper occurred later, in the post-liminal phase, the phase of incorporation, when the marriage was 'solemnised' as an event which had already taken place.

Certainly the idea of marriage as sexual consummation would appear to be secondary to that of an alliance of families. The new state of affairs brought about by the rite between two previously unaligned family and friendship networks is expressed in several dramatic details within the traditional Western marriage service that are often ignored or overlooked. An example of this is the way that bride and groom begin the service standing to left and right respectively - i.e. on the same sides of the church occupied by their own families - and end the service moving across to the opposite sides in order to lead the procession out of church. The procession itself represents the union of the two families, made up as it is of previously unrelated couples now walking together side by side.

Our own understanding of marriage as primarily concerned with the disposition of heart and mind of the two people most directly involved - marriage as a free relationship of adult persons who call on God and his Church to witness to the sanctity of their own privately undertaken mutual gift of themselves - is central to the ritual of a Christian wedding. The act provided by the state for civil marriages, while it reproduces the more public aspects of the ceremony ('I call upon these persons here present, to witness', etc.) lacks the intimacy of the wonderful moment in the Church's service when man and woman make their vows to each other, which is superbly expressed in the Anglican marriage service:

I give you [receive] this ring as a sign of our marriage. With my body I honour you, all that I am I give to you, and all that I have I share with you, within the love of God, Father, Son and Holy Spirit.

This is the most intimate part of the marriage service and repre-sents the liminal phase of the rite. It is the crucial point of change, involving a surrender of selfhood, an abandonment of one's habitu : security that, if properly understood and appreciated, is both difficult and painful to achieve, especially when performed in the presence of others and in so precise and unmistakable a way. Again its unambiguous meaning is brought home by the actual shape of the rite, which falls naturally into the usual three sections:

A. *The pre-liminal phase.*

This is the action of separation that marks what is going to happen as an unique event. It is for purposes of identification and preparation.

1. The purpose and significance of Christian marriage are pointed out, with suitable readings from the Bible.

2. It is announced that this particular couple are to be married.

3. The couple (joined in the Anglican service by the congregation) state that they 'know not of any lawful impediment' to the marriage.[14]

B. *The liminal phase.*

The couple make their promises to each other, facing each other in order to do this. A ring is given and received, or rings are exchanged. The extremely personal nature of the liminal phase is brought home by the symbolism of the ring, which stands for faithfulness and the interchange of love; this is blessed by the priest or minister, and held on the beloved's finger as vows are given and exchanged. The priest may use his stole to bind together the couple's hands. (If there is a need for establishing the civil validity of the marriage during the service itself, as is the case with the Roman Catholic rite, the intimacy of this part of the rite is destroyed by the congregation's being called to witness the vows, a public event which really belongs to the pre-liminal phase.)

C. *The post-liminal phase.*

'In the presence of God and before this congregation, N and N have given their consent and made their marriage vows to each other. They have declared their marriage by the joining of hands and by the giving and receiving of a ring. I therefore proclaim that they are husband and wife.' (The priest joins their right hands together) 'That which God has joined together let not man divide.' Thus in Section 17 of the Marriage Service in the Alternative Service Book the priest states clearly and concisely what has just happened. The division between stages B and C is not so obvious in the Roman Catholic service, although the offering of thanks to God in the final part brings home the fact that something real has been taking place. Some Christians might say that the rite can only really be considered complete when it is followed by, or contained within, the Eucharistic Liturgy. Nevertheless, the Roman Catholic Rite for Celebrating Marriage outside Mass and the corresponding Anglican Marriage Service are genuine rites of passage in themselves. That is, they conform to the outline, and have the impact of such rituals throughout the world. The rite moves inwards to its centre and outwards again, so that the private mutuality of what happens at its heart is unforgettably brought home to all present.

THE FUNERAL
Funerals and the Shape of Human Existence
Throughout their lives, men and women must face situations of personal crisis, some of which cause them so much psychological stress that they are forced to seek medical help of one kind or another, and at these times the assurance of God's sustaining love is most precious to them. Psychological research suggests that the kind of stress that causes personal breakdown is not the continual emotional pressure of a difficult relationship or the nervous energy expended in coping with the demands of a particularly arduous job - these may in fact be the very things that keep us going. The crisis comes not when we are carrying the burden, but when we have to lay it down. We may be longing to be free from the responsibilities and exertions of the task that engages us, so that the yoke chafes more and more and we feel that we can hardly wait for the final blessed moment of release. When we have completed one job, however, we find that another, perhaps harder, project demands our attention. Perhaps we can face this in the same way that we responded to previous challenges, things that were terrifying at first just because they were new and had problems and difficulties we had to find our own way of getting to grips with, but situations that were at least recognisable in terms of a definable challenge to our ingenuity and perhaps endurance. If we can do this without too much personal suffering we are fortunate, for it seems that to be able to transfer one's energies from one task to another in this way is both a gift and a privilege. The challenge that frequently confronts people at such times is much harder to come to terms with.

Quite simply, it is the challenge of not being able to do what we have been doing, even though we may have hated doing it and longed to stop. Not being able to do it ever again. The road we have been travelling along may have had its obstacles and pitfalls, it may from time to time have turned some dangerous corners or even appeared to double back on itself, but looking back it was still recognisably a road. Now it falls away before our feet. What to do now? Which way to go? Is there another road, and if there is, is it one we can take? The state of mind is a familiar one to most of us, and we associate it with those periods of our lives when the pattern of existence has been suddenly and drastically changed. Most characteristically we associate it with times of bereavement and loss involving the death of someone dearly loved by us, but it casts its shadow over every important shift in our outward circumstances, affecting our inward experience of life.

Much of the behaviour that Colin Murray Parkes and John Bowlby vividly describe as being typical of human grieving can be explained in terms of the way in which we seek out the dead in order to have the blessed relief of talking to them again, so that they may really know what we thought and felt about them.[15] The urge to communicate at the deepest most personal level rises to a peak of intensity at such times, which is why so many bereaved people attend seances or turn to spiritualism in order to gain a measure of relief. From this point of view, funeral services are ways in which we renew our shattered relationship with somebody we love, for they enable us to hand our message on to God so that he may 'put the dead person into the picture'. The funeral sets our personal senselessness within the context of a wider sense, easing our intolerable feelings of frustrated impotence when our interior world is shattered by something outside our control - a blow we cannot sustain, a mental and emotional chaos we cannot contain.

The situation is clear enough, after all. We cannot communicate with a dead person unless we can locate them; we cannot locate them until we are able to think about them, and about the circumstances of our own separation from them. Looking at bereaved people it is clear how much this depends on the use of symbolism. At times of critical change, symbols provide us with a way of incorporating the experience of human breakdown within a scheme of reconstruction that involves the eventual restoration of human meaning and purpose. I say human, but this new understanding of life that gives us the courage to go on living is always experienced as a gift from elsewhere. Religious people interpret it as a gift from God, the God who communicates his own being to us in the form of personal meaning - not in words or ideas, but in the experience of relationship itself. This is not any kind of intellectual experience, but it has a noticeable intellectual effect, for we begin to perceive shape where only chaos existed before.

To put this another way: our ability to cope with living depends on our ability to think rationally and straightforwardly about the situation we are in. At times like this the intensity of our feelings makes such thought impossible. In the immediate presence of death, under the impact of loss, who can think about life? It is at this time that the symbol presents itself to us. It is a symbol of reality, not any kind of distortion or evasion. It does not need interpretation, only incorporation. Indeed, this is its specific purpose: to provide a simple, clear, usable image in the midst of perceptual chaos. As such it can be used as a foundation for a new view of life, one that is radically different in content from the old one and yet resembles it from the point of view of being a coherent structure that can be used as a basis for living.

As we have said, the symbol helps us to accept intuitively facts that we cannot accommodate propositionally. Using the language of images rather than articulated ideas it protects as it exposes. In the context of human grief and loss, it takes account of our inability to think through what has happened to us in order to reconstruct an ordered personal universe, while at the same time making us aware of the real state of affairs at a deeper and more immediate level. By doing this it performs an invaluable service for the human spirit, for it manages to undermine the defences that we put up against an unacceptable reality. Certainly we need time to rebuild our shattered universe, but we need the proper materials as well - and the most necessary of these is some kind of awareness of the truth of our new situation. Thrown into confusion by what has happened, we cling to chaos because the prospect of a cosmos that has been so tragically altered can only terrify us; but nobody can build a practicable world on the basis of a lie or an evasion. The symbol helps us towards eventual recovery by filtering its painful light into our self-protective darkness. The new life that emerges may be experienced as drastically reduced or even tragically impoverished, but it will be an authentic kind of existence, founded on something contemporary psychologists would explain in terms of disordered perceptions that are able to organise themselves around a significant 'core percept' - an element within the situation that has sufficient meaning in itself to allow other elements to organise themselves in relation to it.

The core percept is the funeral symbol, or the funeral in its identity as the symbol of an overarching meaning bestowed upon human life and death. The funeral uses the shape of the rite of passage in order to give our thoughts and feelings the direction, and consequently the significance, that they so desperately need, for the shape of the passage rite is specially contrived to express and contain - to embody - the chaos involved in all genuine change that takes place at an existential level. The unique ability of the rite of passage is its power to use chaos in order to express meaning. In the funeral this is most striking, because of the presence of an actual corpse and the need to dispose of it. This, as Malinowski points out, is the most potent symbol of human limitation, and the most eloquent supplication for divine assistance.[16] In its ritual setting, however, it is more than this, for the pre-liminal, liminal and post-liminal funeral rites that exist throughout the world symbolise the whole sequence of denial, chaos and eventual reintegration that characterises the experience of human grieving.

THE LANGUAGE OF FUNERALS
The Motif of Denial

There is a sense in which corporate rituals give symbolic form to behaviour that is felt to be appropriate, but cannot be immediately indulged in by the bereaved themselves. The funeral says what the bereaved would like to say, but cannot find either the words or strength to express while in the state of shock that the event has produced in them. Often, bereaved people feel unready to admit the fact of loss, while knowing at the same time that somehow that fact has to be admitted.

A deep sense of 'the rightness of things' tells us that grief, the sadness of farewell, the confusion of loss are the appropriate reactions to the death of a fellow human being. In retrospect, we are likely to acknowledge that this was in fact the proper way to behave, so that we are no longer ashamed of the strength of our emotions. If, on the other hand, at the time we ourselves were unable to grieve we shall be grateful for the grief of others. At a deep level of consciousness there is the understanding that there must in fact be tears, that what has happened merits or even demands them - hence the Roman actors with their masks of stylised grief.

In fact, however, an immediate reaction of psychological denial would seem to be quite normal, or even inevitable: 'I can't stand what has happened and I don't want to know anything about it' says the bereaved person to the undertaker; and the undertaker takes him at his word and often makes an exceedingly good job of it.

The first part of the threefold funeral rite takes public account of private mechanisms of defence in order to establish the value and purpose of denial at this particular stage of the overall course of grieving. In this way the public acceptance of denial allows the response itself to contribute to the integrity of the funeral process. For example, in order to spare himself pain the mourner will avoid mentioning the name of the loved person who has died, his purpose being to pretend to himself, as far as he may do, that he or she is still alive. In certain funeral rituals throughout the world this quite normal psychological defence measure is included within the corporate ceremonial of the tribe. The purpose now, however, is to proclaim before everybody that there is no longer any point in mentioning the dead person's name, because he or she is no longer alive as a member of the tribe. This public denial constitutes the first stage in the process of the integration of the reality of death within public and private experience. It is, in fact, the first act in an immense corporate drama, whose plot consists of a dismissal, a resulting confusion and a return.

We find this kind of positive denial, denial as part of the rite, in very many places throughout the world. The means used to establish it may sometimes seem a little harsh, but they are to be understood in the light of the whole ritual complex, for, as with all dramas, the end of the story is implicit in its beginning. First of all it is necessary to get rid of the dead person as speedily and as effectively as possible - not through fear, nor for reasons of hygiene, nor for any kind of negative consideration, but for the positive reason that he is going to a better place, a place he himself wishes to go to, a place of new life. Not only this, but he cannot return to play his proper part within the community until he has been through the whole process, acted out his entire role in the complete scenario. Only then will he return, either publicly, as a ghost or an elder, a member of the community of the blessed, influencing the life of the earthly community; or privately, as a reassuring presence within the life of the individual bereaved person. Those developed funeral rituals that Gorer commends because they conform to the pattern of normal grieving ('a formal withdrawal from society, a period of seclusion and a formal re-entry into society')[17] depend upon this mythological scenario of departure and return. The bereaved are allowed to withdraw from society because the dead person himself has departed from the world of men. In order to arrive at his final destination he has had to depart. The possibility of his returning as a benevolent influence depends on his arrival, which in turn is dependent upon his proper departure thither. Dismissal motifs do not exist by themselves, of course. The dead are still seen as existing within the ritual scenario, playing their part within the articulated drama of the complete rite. For the time being, however, they inhabit the 'time-between-times' symbolised by the next ritual motif, that of chaos.

The Motif of Chaos
It is to this part of the rite, its 'symbolic power-house' that students of ritual have paid the most attention. Ritual itself may be regarded as a return to the centre, the origin of life, situated at its heart rather than on the periphery. Nature turns again to its original wholeness in order to enjoy 'the perfection of the beginning of things'.[18] The central part of the rite is

its most sacred movement, imbued as it is with the holiness of the divinity from which it springs and to which it returns. This is the rite's theophany, the point at which divinity enters the creation to transform it. From the point of view of the ritual symbol, the revelation of new life demands the intervention of God himself. This, indeed, is what religion is about; these ideas of life out of death are fundamental to our religious awareness, implying as they inevitably must the action of one who can bring life to the dead and do so in a way that is real and final. Thus the divine intervention is seen as taking place at the juncture of life and death - specifically, in the chaotic state that characterises the rite's central movement, envisaged as a lack of movement, a meaningless absence of purpose and life. Out of this the new life will spring, not of its own instrumentality but through the creative power of Him who moves creation onwards.

The 'myth of the eternal return' inspires religions throughout the world. Everywhere God's action intervenes between past and future to renew and revitalise creation and restore men and women. The restoring power of God is itself a new creation, not to be confused with what went before, yet inescapably related to it as part of the divine purpose sustaining eternity. The rite presents us in a little space with eternity in microcosm, 'the world in a grain of sand'; seed-time and harvest, part of the seasonal activity of God, are held in creative tension, individual and yet distinct. In the rite the separation is itself a recognisable moment, expressing the terms of relationship between what was and what is yet to come - actually embodying it in order to render it unmistakeable and reveal its significance, upon which the reality of life and death, death and life, depends.

Hence the importance of the mythological motif of the return to chaos that characterises so many religious systems and provides the theological explanation of their rites of passage, in which the past is forcibly put to death and the cosmos plunged into confusion. In this creative turmoil, however, men and women find themselves homologised with the divine intention of transformation mediated by the unique funeral symbol, whose three movements unavoidably suggest and involve one another as they speak of death in the language of new life.

The corollary to this, of course, must be that for those who do not experience the renewing action of the ritual, the condition of chaos may prove permanent. The notion of an in-between state that is difficult both to enter and to leave is present in the funeral behaviour of many people, both ancient and modern. It is connected with ideas concerning the existence of a class of dead people who seek vengeance upon their survivors who neglected to give them the benefit of a proper funeral, or to dispose of their mortal remains in an appropriate way. For thousands of years, the belief has existed that the spirits of those whose bodies go unburied wander about the earth seeking rest or intent on mischief of some kind or other. In its primitive form this belief persists in the official religion of some Australian, Melanesian, African and North American peoples. In more highly developed cultures, it inhabits the twilight zone that exists between religion and folklore. It was an article of faith among Aztecs, Chaldeans, Assyrians, Egyptians, Babylonians, Greeks and Romans. Among developed religions, Buddhism, Hinduism, Judaism and Christianity all preach the vital importance of adequate funeralisation of the dead, with varying degrees of explicitness about the penalties involved in disobedience, whether this be the miserable half-life of existence in the Preta-Loka of Buddhists or Hindus, or the ultimate dishonour that Isaiah prophesies for those who are not allowed to rest in peace in their graves Van Gennep[19] is explicit on the subject of the intentions and attitudes of those dead people who return to haunt the living. They are angry because the funeral rites that are their due have been denied them and their purpose is to demand satisfaction from their survivors:

Like children who have not been baptised, named, or initiated, persons for whom funeral rites are not performed are condemned to a pitiable existence since they are never able to enter the world of the dead or to become incorporated in the society established there. These are the most dangerous dead....[20]

The Motif of Reintegration
To fail to allow death the significance of a completed process, the significance bestowed by symbols of unity, is to refuse to accept it as a happening at all. And this, in the language of religious understanding, is to give the dead person nowhere to go - nowhere to go and nothing to be. Ghosts are beings who, because they are 'neither here nor there', are chronically and agonisingly mislocated. The funeral is the means whereby they are kept in the right place, in their proper dimension of being.

In fact, this need not be very far away from the living. The world of the incorporated and established dead may be understood as impinging upon the world of the living, in some cases even overlapping that world. For purposes of social and psychological integration many cultures welcome home the very ghosts whom they have been at such pains to send away. Having formally dismissed them, and thereby given due acknowledgement to their change of status, they can now accord them proper social recognition. Indeed, the presence of the dead becomes an essential part of the corporate life of society. In these 'ghost cultures' the search for new life is socially recognised as an expression of the striving for continuity in human affairs. Those parts of the social cosmos that can only be imagined are sketched in by the bestowal of dignity upon the noble dead. Thus it may be found that the authority of an individual man or woman actually grows after death, so that they can continue to exercise control of whatever goes on in the communities they have unavoidably had to leave. These are certainly not wandering spirits who have lost their way; the power they have is theirs because they have died. In other words it is the power of taboo-holiness, bestowing on them a different order of authority than can be attained by mere living people. At the same time it sets them apart for relationship as well as authority, distinguishing them from all nameless and status-less presences, making them real in the eyes of the living. They must be taken into account, rather than simply guarded against, because they belong to holiness, to a sphere of being that is to be defined specifically in terms of the distance between it and ordinary things.

By the action of dying and being properly buried - or cremated or exposed to nature and the elements - they have asserted both their intimacy and their superiority. They are the spectators who not only see most of the game but control it as well, reaching with power and authority across the grave, bestowing their own special mana or mysterious power on those whom they select as their instruments in this world and successors in the next. Far from being a limitation on human authority this kind of intercourse with the departed is experienced as a gracious bestowal of supernatural dignity on the efforts of ordinary men and women.

In some parts of the world, then, the ghostly realm serves to complement the world of men and women, giving dramatic form to the creative opposition that exists between the ideal and the real. The relationship is beneficial for both sides: everyday practice and particular enactment give the religious sphere a powerful influence in ordinary secular affairs; normal life gains significance from its metaphysical implications. The interchange is carefully regulated, however, so that in all practical matters the lead is taken by the living, who, after all, are responsible for the privileges enjoyed by the departed in the after-world, as they are in charge of the rites that admit them to it.

The gate between the two worlds is vigorously guarded: those on either side must be allowed to meet, but prevented from mingling. The rite is specifically designed for this purpose. It does so in its own characteristic way by taking account of the confusion it confronts and by so doing transforming it. The pre-liminal rite opens the way up for the dead into the afterlife and the post-liminal one firmly closes it again behind them. In between, however, the two worlds are mingled in chaos.

This chaos is vital, however - necessary to life itself, fundamental to the experience upon which our ordinary reality is founded. It would be a pity if our modern funerals gave no indication of the chaos that forms the background to the ordered arrangements we make to cope with life and death and that gives them their particular meaning and significance. These things have a way of making themselves felt however hard we try to control them and 'keep them in their place' (particularly if we refuse to give them one). No wonder that stories about ghosts and vampires possess such a haunting resonance and that the experience of bereavement often carries with it the uncanny feeling that the dead person is still with us. This may be a comforting experience, cushioning our grief. Often it is characterised by a sense of wrongness. Somehow or other we know he or she should not be here. Not like this, anyway. We feel alarmed, and not a little guilty - perhaps someone has left the door open ... perhaps it was me....

In the last part of the threefold rite of passage, the action of reaching out towards an ultimate completeness and perfection of life possesses a particular vividness, as the movement here is specifically out of chaos and into integration and wholeness. The disunity is of two kinds: an emotional turmoil and an equally disruptive intellectual confusion and alienation. Through the cathartic impact of its scenario, and its ability to involve its participants in an ideal world of personal relationships, the rite acts as a salve for both conditions. Thus the rite is functional and structural, a strictly practical model of the preconditions for reconciliation.

Intra-psychic conflict is here viewed in terms of social interaction. The individual is reached through his relationship with those in his family, tribe or nation. The social organism comes together to bring relief to one of its members, and in so doing reinforces its solidarity. As with marriage ceremonies, funerals may reveal the presence of all sorts of ancient antagonisms and scarcely hidden resentments, but the sense of belonging, of fundamental identity, is implicit in the action of coming to the funeral at all. To attend an enemy's funeral, or one at which enemies will be present, constitutes a significant gesture of reconciliation. As we have seen, the possibility of the presence of all kinds of underlying conflicts is accounted for in the provisions of the central section where quarrels of a long standing kind are symbolically recognised and laid to rest. Here, however, in the final section, the rite reveals its primary purpose. This is not simply the restoration of order out of chaos, but the creation of a new kind of order, one founded upon the honest acceptance of the hard facts about discontinuity. Just as the chaos is real, in the sense that its mythological portrayal in the rite refers directly to the living experience of bereaved men and women, so the final stage of the funeral process, in which the dead are seen as having arrived at their destination, calls for a real acceptance on the part of their survivors of the factual nature of this separation. The rite proposes that the only beneficial relationship between the living and the dead is one in which their separation is mutually acknowledged and officially ratified. In its demythologised form, this may be taken to mean that the possibility of healthy readjustment to normal living on the part of the bereaved depends upon their acceptance of the reality of their loss - an opinion frequently expressed by those who write about bereavement from a psychotherapeutic point of view.

Thus the funeral process presents the reality of emotional deprivation and loss within a framework of meaning and value. There is no immediate escape from pain, for the loss is still there and must be faced by the survivors, but the process of recovery is aided by the assertion of an underlying meaning. Whether this meaning is regarded in terms of the ascription of an ultimate value to human relationship itself, or whether it takes the form of a religious doctrine about the metamorphosis of individual and society through the transforming contact with holiness believed to take place when, in the presence of death, we are totally subordinated to divine power, the result is the same. The final stage of the funeral is intended to embody two mutually contradictory, but equally essential, propositions about death and bereavement: that the dead have been totally separated from the living in a way that is completely irreversible, but that those forces within the human environment that promote and encourage personality, forces inevitably associated with the fact of relationship, have none the less triumphed. The image of a journey between two discrete states of being expresses this problem, and its solution in the rite, most clearly. The states of being are quite distinct. Separated by formlessness and chaos, they do not touch each other at any point. Nevertheless, they are presented here in the context of a proclamation about the victory of the forces of life. Despite its incidental hazards, the journey whose conclusion is signalled by the last stage of the rite is a triumphant one.

In those places where the extended rite of passage is still used for funerals, the reaction of the individual mourner is modified by the cultural attitude to death. People remark on the fact that 'the old funeral movements' affect those who are too stunned or too desolated to know what is happening to them.[21] The chaos of the rite's central section allows such people to ventilate the full force of their grief in the most uninhibited way. Carried along by the rite's course, they are instructed to grieve, and then, at a given moment, once the final phase has been arrived at, they are ordered to stop doing so. In embracing the social obligation to mourn, they are presented with an equally powerful sanction for emergence from grief. Custom demands that the 'valley of the shadow' should be entered, and passed through; it is equally insistent, however, that when the time comes it shall be left behind. Indeed, the integrity of the ritual process ensures that this shall be so. The experience of mourners suggests that this 'social permission to recover from grief' is as vital for the recovery of a sense of purpose in living as was the 'social permission to grieve'.

5

Passage Rite and Sacrament

We have already looked at the two sacraments of baptism and marriage from the point of view of their roles as rites of passage. What about the others? What is the relationship of the passage rite to the sacramental principle in general? From the point of view of the role they play in the life of Christians, one of initiation into deeper involvement with God and consequently a higher kind of personal being, the Christian sacraments can be plainly seen to be rites of passage. That is, they signify the attainment of important stages in our lives and give us continuing support of the most vital kind for the spiritually hazardous journey through life. The particular quality of the support they give us is very important, as is the way in which they give it, for this is the kind of enlightenment and refreshment that can really only be mediated by rituals. These are not simply ideas in picture form, but real personal events: the experience of life in the ordinary everyday world of people and things is illuminated by a vision of divine reality - or of ordinary reality transfigured by divinity - that answers our questions about the meaning of life and death and draws us closer to one another.

In sacramental ritual the tokens of our participation in God and one another are the very stuff of our common experience of the world; water, fire, food, blood, flesh, secular things made holy by acting as the mediums for our return to God. Similarly, the movements and gestures of the rite communicate the message of reconciliation in the most direct and immediate way. They are the language of a humanity shared with us by God himself. The aspiration towards personal wholeness is a movement upwards and outwards: upwards towards a superior essence, outwards towards a better existence, a more satisfactory way of living in the world with other people. We discover that an increased capacity for using the things that happen to us in this world, whatever they may be as ways of attaining greater personal holiness, can only come about by personal contact with someone who has made the greatest human change, faced and survived the greatest human crisis of all, and now holds out his hand to us. Someone who by his action and in his person, makes sense of our world. Thus belief in God, and experience of personal encounter with him, find their expression in the shape of a perfect action, the expression of being that is given and received in the interchange of love.

For Christians the sacraments are more than rituals. They are the Church itself, for the Christian Church is the common life of the persons, divine and human, who constitute it. It has been suggested that, when it comes down to it, the way in which the Church exists in the world is not by agreeing to a set of theological principles, but by participating in a succession of ritual actions that symbolise a co-inherence and communion of persons much profounder than any collaboration of ideas or attitudes of mind. The experience of sharing a common identity is realised in every Christian sacrament. Sacramental holiness is profoundly personal though, because the rite brings us into relationship with the divine person who chooses to live among us according to the manner of our own humanity: not only psychologically, according to the relationship of individuals in society, but biologically, according to the rules of our actual physical existence, depending upon the food and drink which keep our bodies going, and upon which every other kind of human experience necessarily depends. Similarly, the events represented in the sacrament are believed to be matters of real history, things that have taken place in ordinary human time. The miracle of the sacrament itself is tangible (as well as audible and visible), because it takes place in the present and recreates the past, and yet it is truly miraculous, it really reveals and presents God, because it reveals the eternal in history. In every way, then, the rite's symbolism takes the things of man and uses them for our immediate participation in God himself. Because these things include pain, destruction and death, they, too, are included in, and transformed by, the rite of passage.

It is hard to see how any rite of passage could avoid the subject of death, because every real human change is a kind of dying, and dying itself is the experience of change with which rites of passage must necessarily concern themselves if they are to be of any real use at all to men and women. Certainly if the rite is to be used as a way of lifting us up to God, then it must make a breach in the toughest barrier of all, our finite human existence. The cross of Christ, the symbol of a death that is the gateway from life to life, stands at the centre of every Christian sacrament, uniting them into a complete scheme of rites of passage and giving each of them the power to reflect the others while performing their own specific role within the whole series. Just as the parts of the rite imply one another, so each individual sacrament is at one and the same time pre-liminal, liminal and post-liminal. Because of the dominant symbolism of the death and resurrection of Christ, all are essentially liminal rites. Some, however, stress this nature more than others.

Baptism, marriage and ordination, for instance, are obvious thresholds. The Eucharist, on the other hand, may at first seem to be post-liminal because it is so clearly the celebration of something that has already been achieved (as, indeed, are penance and also the sacrament of healing). At the same time, it is unmistakably the liminal presence of the cross and the prefiguring of the Eschaton. Ecclesiastical tradition regards both baptism and confirmation as pre-liminal to the Eucharist. Again, the presence of the cross makes this a practical consideration rather than a theological necessity. All preserve the shape of the rite of passage in their individual structures, moving inwards and away from the central timeless moment of the sacramental action itself, despite the fact that their theological meaning transcends any such division. Obviously the Eucharist itself is not a rite of passage in the sense that it marks a particular stage in an individual's progress through life; at the same time it provides us with a recurrent source of 'food for the journey' of an essential kind, preserving us in our identity as voyagers. As such it certainly belongs to the thinking associated with such rituals.

The exact theological purpose and ecclesiastical significance of individual sacraments has changed both in the Roman Catholic and Anglican Churches, largely in accordance with shifting social circumstances. There is greater encouragement of adult baptism and less separation between baptism and confirmation, which can no longer be seen as any kind of separate rite of passage. In both Churches the motif of setting apart candidates for ordination to constitute a special holy caste distinct from the royal priesthood of 'ordinary' Church members has been modified by the influence of a richer understanding of the doctrine of the Body of Christ. Roman Catholics are living through changes in the traditional forms of both penance and the sacrament of healing, in the general direction of making both less formal and occasion-specific (for example, healing no longer implies the imminence of actual physical death.) In line with the requirements of a less rigidly structured, more mobile society the Christian sacraments are being used in a more flexible, more imaginative way. In accordance with the sheer speed of the changes happening in the lives of individuals and groups, a Catholic scholar refers to 'a unified sacramental discipline'[1] of Baptism, Confirmation and Eucharist, bringing together three sacraments in one comprehensive passage rite, not all the parts of which are to be celebrated together, certainly, but that definitely holds together in the thinking and teaching of the Church. This is a powerful way of expressing the sheer thrust of the happening that is taking place, the immensity of the transformation involved.

Yet each sacrament has an equally powerful dynamism of its own, pivoting upon its central timelessness, drawing us from the past and impelling us towards the future. We have already seen this with regard to baptism. In the traditional form of confirmation the rite begins with a pre-liminal phase in which those about to be confirmed are required to make their own personal statement of allegiance to Christ and renunciation of evil, and to receive exorcism from the power of Satan by being anointed with consecrated oil; then comes the climax when the bishop lays his hand on each individual and invokes the effective presence of the Holy Spirit; finally those who have been confirmed are received back into the congregation in a post-liminal ceremony of welcome. In ordination, those about to be ordained move out from the congregation to be presented to the bishop, who lays upon them the charge of carrying out their future role with the grace of God and to the best of their ability. However this is performed at various times and in various churches, it is always followed by a movement outwards, as the new deacon or priest assumes his or her role. Here as in other rituals of change the idea of what is to happen dictates the order of events, and it is certain to go on doing so whatever liturgical revisions take place, so long as biblical narrative determines the form of the central symbolic action. With regard to healing the biblical directions are quite clear and suggest a rite in which oil is blessed in advance, prayers and anointing take place and the sick person is given holy communion to provide strength for the journey onwards. The event requires its own inalienable shape in order to establish its completeness, a state of affairs that stands out clearly in the sacrament of forgiveness, as the penitent searches his or her conscience, makes his or her confession, carries out his or her penance.

The most obvious correspondence between the sacraments and other religious rituals of separation, transition and incorporation lies in their use at particular times in the life-history of individuals and communities as ways of crossing specific thresholds. In this way, human life is seen by the Church as a succession of initiations that, because they are brought about by participation in the saving acts of Christ, are also consummations. The Christian community, the people of God, the New Israel, sanctified by the indwelling Spirit of Christ celebrates each stage in its corporate journey through time, refreshing men and women at the crisis of personal existence with deep draughts of immortality. In addition, the personal time-span of each individual Christian is marked off by similar rites of passage as our creaturely nature is restored to its original divine value and significance in holy baptism and confirmation, our adulthood in Christian marriage and our death in the sacrament of healing and the viaticum. Thus the sacramental journey of a Christian man or woman through life makes a complete sequence, an extended rite of passage, beginning with pre-liminal rites, passing through liminal and post-liminal ones, and returning to the final initiation.

In this way, what has been said here about rites in general applies with particular force to the sacraments. Vehicles of a unique revelation, they make use of human creativeness in order to symbolise divine creation, all that it demands and all that it bestows. They are a representation of the world as God intends it to be, the paradise destroyed by mankind's selfishness and disobedience and restored by God's redeeming love. They are not just pictures of this perfection, visual aids to serve as models for living and dying in the right way, for they are able to speak for us as well as to us and about us. Bodily movement and spiritual intention are united here as nowhere else in human life, issuing in a communication of irresistible forcefulness, for the human body has a realism that no idea can ever possess. This remains the case whether the movement is that of the priest who elevates the host in the sanctuary of the great cathedral, or of the patient in the hospital ward who reaches out a feeble hand for the sacrament and has to be helped by the nurse, only to drop it on the pillow.

The action the sacraments embody is our own, given to us for our life and our joy in the world that is and our co-operation with Christ in bringing to birth the world that shall be. The love that begets them is the love that speaks forth from the pages of the Old and New Testaments, the intensely personal love of Yahweh for Israel, so movingly expressed by Jeremiah and Second Isaiah and the anguished devotion of Hosea. It is the love Jesus describes in the Beatitudes and elsewhere as the very essence of blessedness, the costly love of humility and service that shares in the nature of God himself, who 'wants no-one to be lost and everyone to be saved'.[2] It is the love that inherits the world God made, and continues to make, by expressly countermanding the principles that selfishness holds to be the necessary conditions for human survival in the world: 'If I do not wash you, you are not in fellowship with me.'[3]

This is not to say of course that, because our sacramental life contains within it the possibility of such perfection, it cannot be perverted and maimed by human sinfulness. To cling to sacramental grace in a selfish way is effectively to cut oneself off from it by one's own actions and to run the risk of trying to restrict God's love in order to enjoy it all oneself. This is a refusal to accept grace as a gift and a determination to manipulate the giver in accordance with one's own purposes. It is the distortion of freedom in the name of selfishness that we call sin, an expression of the fundamental distortion at the root of all human life. It is certainly not confined to lay Christians. As we all know to our cost, it is all too easy for clergy to use this precious gift of God as a kind of bribe instead of the pledge of a real communion of hearts and minds, of lives: a true meeting of people in the depths and heights of personhood. In other ways, too, the rite can be assaulted: by clinging intentionally to bitterness and resentment in the place devoted to reconciliation and forgiveness; by refusing to concentrate properly on what is happening, as if it were an automatic ratification of everything you yourself are, and all that you stand for, rather than a searchingly personal encounter with the Lord of Life, who holds our very being in his hands. We are still free, even in the focussed presence of God. We can still sin, perhaps more awfully here than anywhere else.

Most of the time, thank God, we do not want to - and so we usually do not. Conscious of what is at stake, of the divine possibility opened up to us, we do our best to surrender to the loving demand of Christ. Jesus said 'by gaining his life a man will lose it; by losing his life, for my sake, he will gain it'.[4] In the sacraments the interchange of love, which is the triune being of God himself, is imaged forth in actions of self-surrender, as men and women reach out away from themselves towards the other in accordance with an economy that is the opposite of normal commercial activity, for the action of receiving life involves a surrender to the giver that is the greatest gift of which we are capable. We do not give in order to receive, but receive in order to give. Nor does the gift of love know any barriers. Human ideas about worthiness stand in the way of God's intention. More than that, they blasphemously impugn the generosity of his action, the universality of his acceptance, for 'there is no question here of Greek and Jew, circumcised and un-circumcised, barbarian, Scythian, freeman, slave; but Christ is all, and is in all'.[5] All that God requires is a heart eager to give thanks, or to be able to give thanks, and a willingness to confess the need for personal assistance in living, however the need is expressed, whatever it is and whoever expresses it. We are told plainly that those whose need is greatest, who are suffering hardships of body, mind or spirit, must be heard first, for 'anything you did for one of my brothers here, however humble, you did for me'.[6] All this is symbolised most powerfully in the Eucharist.

The Eucharist as Rite of Passage

Can our discussion about rites of passage contribute to our appreciation of the significance of the central Christian sacrament? I believe that it can. The Eucharist is the rite of passage for the whole journey taking account of all human life, applicable to every stage and all situations. The Eucharist is the rite of passage for our moments and our days - for how we are living now, not how we have lived.

The life we share with God, the life by which in Jesus Christ we participate in the Father and the Holy Spirit, is the life of people in relationship. Christ proclaims this fact in the revelation of his own presence; for where Christ is, there is the relationship of people, the community of Love. It could be said that the principles according to which the Eucharist is organised constitute the underlying structure of personhood itself, for they correspond to the action of self-giving whereby the individual becomes the person, moving out of isolation into community. The action of abandoning the self for the other, the glorious primal movement - original and inevitable when it happens in God, for it is the expression of his joy in the nature of his being, but difficult and terrifying for men and women, as for the Son who took their nature upon himself - is eternally presented in the Eucharist. It is presented to us not as an idea or a proposition, but as a living event in which we are ourselves deeply and essentially involved: a fact, the fact, of our common life.

In the Eucharist the life of an individual is taken, broken and shared among men and women. His individuality is of the greatest importance. He is not any kind of corporate identity, but a specific person, a Hasidic prophet from a Galilean village. Although he is a member of the Jewish people, he does not represent them. His rabbinic status is unofficial and his legal position ambiguous. He is not any kind of solid citizen, but a social outcast and the friend and companion of outcasts. His words and deeds proclaim him as one who stands over against organised society, seeking - and needing - human companionship, but unwilling to collude with the social consensus in its repression of the individual. For he *is* the individual. It follows from this, of course, that he is *this* individual, for even at this stage we cannot generalise about him. The human truth about God is this particular man, in this place, at this time.

Theologically, of course, Jesus 'stands for' every man and woman in his or her situation in life; but that is the language of our thought about him, not of our embodied experience. It is the specificity of Jesus that is precious to us, for it is his individual personhood to which we relate as people. This fact is the subject matter of the whole of the first part of the Mass. The ministry of the word is the action of distinguishing this man, identifying him as the one whose life is foretold in the Old Testament and described in the Epistles and the Gospel.

It is our relationship with him as a person that moves us to confess our sins and lay bare to God the most painful secrets of our hearts, and our understanding of the meaning of his personhood that orders the assertions we make about ultimate reality and divine truth in the creed. It is through him that we intercede for the men and women in the world, commending each one to God in and through the personhood of Christ. This is the one body that is broken on the cross, as the one loaf is broken at the Eucharist and the one life shared among many in the communion. It is in his or her individuality that each person received the whole being of God, the fullness of Christ. The fullness is the common life of individuals, the authentic life of personhood that is always corporate. Thus, the Eucharist moves from the existence of Christ as a particular human being to the common life of his mystical body, through the action of dissolution and disintegration, according to which the single one sacrifices his own organic unity, his identity as a separate individual human being, in order to take it up again in a new more perfect form as a person living in the fullness of divine love with other people. He who is relationship, freedom and love separates himself from his own true being by embracing the existential isolation of the single member of an alienated race in order to transform the isolation of individuals into the relationship of genuine persons. Incarnation and atonement are the same loving gesture of God in Christ, and their meaning and purpose is the transformation of the world by the reconciliation of separate and distinct human beings with God and one another, so that they may grow in one another's sight, reflecting one another's individual being and reinforcing one another's personhood, shaping one another to the likeness of the Son of God.[7] The Eucharist makes use of the shape of the rite of passage with its clear division into three movements of separation, transition and incorporation: 'taking', 'breaking', and 'sharing'. Its purpose also is that of the rite, for it is both initiatory and unitive, enabling those who are reborn in Christ's death and resurrection to grow in his image and likeness.

Indeed, the shape of the Eucharist is the shape of the experience of Christians, whose life in the Body of Christ passes through stages of vocation, justification and sanctification.[8] By its action of initiating us into the death and resurrection of Christ, the Eucharist delivers us from the fatal consequences of our individual tendency to commit sins by rescuing each of us from the law that, because of our personal weakness, is for us 'the power of sin'.[9] Thus it is a force in the world for personal transformation at the deepest level of our being. Indeed, as the sacrament of unity, it is concerned with the corporate struggle of the Body of Christ against evil on a cosmic scale, the Satanic use of structures to enslave individuals and entire communities and to produce personal alienation by societal means. In the Eucharist as rite of passage, 'union' and 'initiation' are clearly shown to be interdependent ideas, for not only is initiation an experience or an action that leads into a condition of union with others, but the celebration in the Eucharist of an essential unity in Christ is a progressive initiation. This fact about Christians becomes more and more evident in their experience of and behaviour in the world.

To see the Eucharist as a rite of passage is to begin to understand how extremely practical it is. Both the Eucharist itself and the ordinary daily life of Christians who participate in and are changed by it, are events taking place in the world in order to transform the native quality and conditions of its life. The purpose of the sacraments is to create the social organism of the kingdom of God on earth. In this sense the Eucharist is a political action, establishing a society totally opposed to the principles according to which the world is organised, principles of human self-assertion, self-justification, self-protection, self-conservation. It carries within itself the power to transform human society in the only way and at the only level that society can effectively be transformed, the level of personal relationships, which is the authentically human level. Christ's own presence at the heart of the sacrament is the triumph of divine personhood, which results in the making of people who are in Christ and participate in his victories over the idolatries that strike at the root of our freedom to respond lovingly and creatively - idolatries of the world, the flesh and the devil. The Eucharist is God's action taken against the depersonalising effect of life in a 'godless' society, for it is the pledge of our divine-human solidarity, the action that establishes and celebrates our unique personhood within the transformed society of the People of God.

At the same time, however, like all corporate rituals, the Eucharist represents our human understanding of the state of affairs confronting us with regard to the arrangements to be made for carrying on our daily lives in the world. As we have seen, religious rituals are not the spontaneous outpouring of social or religious idealism, or of any other kind of feeling, but are very consciously contrived artefacts, possessing an obvious social purpose - that of facilitating crucial changes within the social experiences of individual members of a community. The rite of passage demonstrates the artificial nature of social structures in the most dramatic way, for it presents them as inferior approximations of a perfect society, one which in terms of present reality does not exist, but is none the less believed to be possible. Ritual does not express an innate social holiness, as Durkheim maintains. Rather it is a tool men and women use to make their social arrangements more holy by bringing them face to face with the image of an ideally structured community. The idea of perfection is passed back and forth among the participants in the ritual exchange and grows by being shared. To this extent the rite improves reality by making it more like the perfection it imitates. The message of the rite is about a holiness that comes to men and women, not one that they already possess as a characteristic of their own ways of acting. Victor Turner has written powerfully and at length on the significance of ritual as a tool for changing the attitudes, ideas and feelings of individuals and causing new social groupings to emerge and existing structures to be drastically altered. The reconciliation of individuals, and the revision and reshaping of personal loyalties, which is facilitated in and inspired by the ritual event, is no mere social palliative. Indeed, the course of history itself is changed by the kind of social action presented by ritual, which serves to crystallise all kinds of ideas and feelings that would not otherwise achieve the form and definition belonging to action in the world. Ritual is an example of the involvement of ideas in action. It is no mere aesthetic exercise. It possesses the form of art, but its purpose is to change, not merely to reflect, the way people think, feel and behave.[10]

It is important to recognise the fact that the rite's artificial nature is not disguised. In rites throughout the world the theatricality of the proceedings is more often proclaimed than concealed, for what is aimed at is an acted demonstration of the artificial nature of human social arrangements, which can only really be seen in their true identity as the creations of men and women when they are set within the context of an ideal perfection. In corporate rituals a religious presence demonstrates the contingent nature of secular society. The ordering of relationship between individuals that constitutes social structure is shown to be a human imitation of perfection, something standing over and against the ideal condition to which it aspires. The arrangements for social interaction that exist may appear to be the best that can be managed, but even these need to be authenticated by contact with divine perfection. As it stands, society itself is demonstrably not holy enough. The rite reveals it as something that continually needs to be strengthened, encouraged and endorsed by infusions of holiness. It is this holiness that is called upon to provide the means whereby an individual may be enabled to surmount successive crises in his or her passage through life. At every stage on the way, divinity is invoked to make good the deficiencies of humanity and the distinction clearly made between God's intention and the real situation existing among men and women. For all its aspiration towards holiness, human society remains imperfect, changeable, contingent. Such is the message and action of the rite, which exorcises the effects of the process of social alienation by which society itself is deified.

Nowhere is all this more apparent than in the Eucharist, the central sacrament of Christians. The Eucharist is the assertion of true holiness, the celebration of the kingship of God and the proclamation of his kingdom on earth. Just as it is the realisation of our union with God in Christ, so it is the action whereby Christ exorcises the evil that exists in human society. All sin is social, for it affects the relationship between a particular human individual and every other person, whether divine or human.

The kind of Satanic evil that is directly exorcised by the Eucharistic action is societal rather than social. Certainly it involves individual sinfulness, but it goes considerably beyond this, for its action is expressed not in the weakness and corruptibility of human nature, but in its negation and denial as a result of the total breakdown of relationship. If, as Harvey Cox suggests, the task of the Christian Church is to be a 'cultural exorcist',[11] then the Eucharist is central to this task because it presents the people of God as a living community, gathered together in their most characteristic attitude around the table of the Lord. The Eucharistic event symbolises the essence of the new creation of Christ Jesus, for it both expresses and realises the terms of its existence in the world.

The Eucharist is the sacrament of individuals-in-community, which is another way of saying that it is the sacrament of true personhood. The action of participation in the personhood of Christ defines and establishes our own personality. As we become more like him, so we become more truly ourselves, because it is his wholeness as a person to which we are conformed by the Eucharistic action. This is the central fact about our membership of the sacramental community, for it is the fact on which the community itself is founded, the rock upon which the Church is built. Community, the reality of personal sharing, can only exist where individuals are able to be themselves - and able to be honest about their own feelings and motives, able to contribute their own ideas and skills, not needing to flatter or placate others, seeking always to keep faith with God in Christ Jesus. The integrity of the community depends on the integrity of each member, for each individual can only help build up the family of individuals when he himself is strong enough to take up his cross and give himself away to the other in love. Thus the strength of personal being that is given by participation in Christ through the initiatory sacraments to individuals is the life that sustains the entire community: individuality allows Eucharist just as Eucharist promotes individuality, by realising that eternal unity of the divine life that consists in the free interchange of selves.

As the sacrament of the common life in the Body of Christ, the Eucharist refutes once and for all the argument that dominates human thinking about society, according to which the individual man or woman is perpetually set over against the collectivity, so that personal freedom and corporate responsibility come to be regarded as irreconcilable opposites. In this Eucharistic community we discover the freedom to be truly ourselves. In company with every other manifestation of Satan's power to use human ingenuity against itself this particular idea, too, has been 'nailed to the Cross of Christ'.[12] Just as, through the action of the Holy Spirit at large in the world, Christ redeems and renews every single aspect of the personal life of men and women, so this divinely established Eucharistic society exorcises the characteristic human function of social organisation, thus allowing human beings to live together in that quality of mutual love that is the uniquely Christian way of being in the world. As the meaning of each of the sacraments is summed up, and their effect perpetuated, in the Eucharistic sacrifice, so it recapitulates their specific function as rites of passage whereby the social and religious identity of individuals and societies is established and confirmed. The sacrament of the Church's identity in the world of space and time, the Eucharist is the unfailing source of refreshment for every Christian in his or her passage through life.

Appendices

Appendix A

Marking the Way

Perhaps rites of passage may be used to help more people to come to terms with change. For various reasons - perhaps some of those mentioned in the Introduction, perhaps simply because of 'the speed of modern life' - this vital resource has fallen out of use during the last few centuries and needs to be revived. We have seen that the shape of the rite is fundamental to many traditional Church services. Perhaps this can be extended and more services provided along these lines, so that particular events in the lives of individuals or groups of people can be celebrated in this time-honoured way. Apart from extending the liturgical repertoire - which would surely be no bad thing from the point of view of the relevance of what goes on in church to those who regularly attend services - even more importantly people who are not Church members might find real encouragement from a more flexible approach to liturgy, one that takes individual needs more seriously by showing concern for the circumstances according to which people's lives are actually being lived - something more personal, in other words.

From one point of view the time would certainly seem to be ripe for liturgical change. Thanks to the Charismatic Movement, congregations have become used to forms of service that are more free-flowing, less rigidly structured. Whatever the service may be, it is likely to be more immediate, less 'stuffy' than before. We look at people nowadays and talk to them during the service; sometimes we even touch them! Unfortunately the movement towards greater spontaneity, necessary though this is for the achievement of change in worship, has not yet reached the point at which the structures of services have been really affected. They have been

neglected, even abused, but not changed. We are still in the chaos
section of liturgical growth, awaiting the emergence of significant
structure for future life. If our worship is to be truly expressive of an
incarnate faith, it must have shape. Its meaning must be incarnated in
expressive action.

The following services are examples of my own experimenting in
this direction. They are passage rites that have been specially constructed
to fit particular pastoral situations. It will be seen that they are not
particularly free in form. Even though they are intended to be regarded as
sketches, or suggestions, rather than blue-prints, a definite effort has been
made in all four to preserve the all-important tripartite shape of the rite,
upon which so much of its meaning depends. Modern social conditions
usually require a single service rather than the three separate but related
ones described by van Gennep. However it is feasible to include all three
ritual movements of the passage rite within a single ceremony, as the ritual
complexes described by anthropologists are really expanded instances of
a single event itself falling inevitably into three stages, reproducing the
shape of significant changes that occur in the lives of individuals and
societies. This fact became obvious when we examined the Christian
sacraments from the point of view of their basic structure and saw how
each revolved around a central symbolic action into which the rite led and
from which it proceeded.

1.   The pre-liminal phase identifies the theme, separating this event from
all others and stating the intention of the whole service. It may be verbally
expressed or presented in pictorial or dramatic form, or contain readings
from the bible or other literature, accompanied perhaps by expressive
music. Ideally it would involve some kind of exploration of the way things
are now, in particular: What is good and valuable about the present
situation? What do we want to carry with us on our journey? What do we
want to jettison? What is our hope for the future? It is essential to be clear
and honest about these things. This section culminates in a corporate
declaration of intentions and aspirations.

2.   The liminal phase of the rite signifies disintegration. In this section the
congregation move deeper into the actual experience that is the theme of
the rite. This will be more symbolic than the previous section and should
not hesitate to portray the pain and confusion undergone by the rite's
protagonist as a result of the present crisis. One of the themes might be
human loneliness in the midst of troubles of a profoundly personal nature.
The keynote of the section is confusion and disorganisation. At such times
men and women are lonely, frail and lost. They do not know which way

to turn. This central movement is the most difficult to arrange, as most people are embarrassed by the idea of having to reveal such feelings - or any feelings - in public, particularly during a Church service. On the other hand, even the least degree of self-disclosure in public is likely to prove a very painful experience, certainly suitable for this part of the service - and the symbolic nature of the action is specifically designed to reveal and protect at the same time.

3. The post-liminal phase is the final part of the ritual where whatever has emerged of newness and life is celebrated, and established as part of the state of affairs now existing as a result of the rite; the spiritual renewal that comes about as a result of having participated in and survived pain, particularly when it is shared. The rite's symbolism has mediated the presence of suffering at an intuitive, non-thetic level, allowing it to be acknowledged and shared, a burden to be borne by the whole congregation, enabling them to take it upon themselves and offer it to God as an action of renewal and corporate reintegration. The post-liminal movement is celebrated by all present with music and singing, dances and prayers, as the mood of the rite shifts again, moving outwards from the central point of change to the affirmation of new life.

The religious nature of such a service may be explicit or implicit: it may include hymns, prayers and bible readings or not, according to circumstances. It does not need to be as dramatic as I have suggested here so long as it reproduces in some way and to some extent the original shape of the rite of passage on which it is based. Not only intense personal experiences provide suitable occasions for the rite. Any intention of human aspiration, any experience of change and hope for renewal, however ordinary, is properly expressed according to the fundamental model of human transformations presented by the language of the rite.

Finally, it seems to me that, using the framework set out above, rites of a sacramental kind - baptisms, ordinations, services of divine healing - could be put together to be both relevant to the needs of contemporary men and women and yet carry all the ancient power of the rite of passage to symbolise personal change in an unforgettable way. The rite provides revelation with its most eloquent language for practical living: over the ages its message continues to move us.

The following services are reasonably conventional in content, in that they use hymns, set prayers and bible readings; they even contain short homilies. None of these things is very important, however, at least not in the form in which they have been set down here. In fact the services could be completely wordless. They could depend on the use of dance or mime to put their message across or use visual display or creative lighting and expressive music. Perhaps they would be better if they did, because words, even the beautiful words of some of the prayers included here, may distract from the immediate impact of acted symbolism. In the rite of passage it is what happens that counts; and what happens comes across in terms of the order of events.

In these services the shape of the rite is marked by the use of hymns. It could be done by a startling change of lighting, or the use of a drum, or any number of ways that might be thought both effective and suitable for the occasion. On the other hand, the hymn's content itself contributes to the meaning of the rite, apart from providing an unmistakable structural element. The disadvantage of familiar prayers and hymns is that they may have lost some of the immediacy they possessed when we first heard them. (Sometimes they touch the right nerve and then the result is unforgettable.) In any case, they are always to be preferred to extemporised expression for the obvious reason that the rite demands clarity and directness - its effects are focussed and its message precise.

Appendix B

Preparing for the Birth of a Child

All: (Hymn) Praise the Lord, Ye Heavens Adore Him.
Minister: God created man in his own image, male and female created he them.
The Lord be with you.
All: And also with you.
Minister: Heavenly Father, you make all things, sharing your creation with us. Bless this man and woman in all the fullness of their mutual joy. Help them now as they prepare to open their hearts in welcome to the child who is soon to join them.

A member of the congregation reads a passage chosen by the couple. This should express the joy they have in each other's company, referring perhaps to shared interests or pursuits (this could be danced or mimed). A bible passage celebrating the joy of human love may be read (e.g. The Song of Solomon). .

Minister: Helen is going to have a baby, and she and Tony rejoice and give thanks to God. There is nothing so marvellous as a new life, nothing lifts the heart so much as this does. This will be their baby, God's blessing on a unique relationship. In every relationship of love there are special things that only the lovers know. These and new ones like them must be shared now, and this will not always be easy, because new life is precisely what it says - new life. We have met to give Tony and Helen an opportunity to say goodbye to one life before they welcome another [Here the minister may describe some of the interests and activities that give the couple's life together its particular character. Words are not really necessary for much of this part of the service, either. The essential thing is to build up a picture of the relationship as it is now.]

Parents-to-Be: Lord God, our heavenly Father, we thank you for the love you have given us to share.

All: Lord God, we thank you.

Parents-to-Be: Lord God, we thank you for your promise of new life in the future.

All: Lord God, we thank you.

Parents-to-Be: Help us, Lord, to bring up this child in ways of faith and hope and love, for everything we have is yours, and our joy is only in your service.

All: Lord God, we thank you.

(Hymn) Make me a channel of your peace.

After this hymn the parents-to-be join hands and walk down through the congregation and back again up into the sanctuary. While moving down towards the back of the church they are taking note of their friends in the pews, shaking hands, embracing, kissing people. On the journey back they remain silent all the way. Reaching the sanctuary they move apart so that they are standing facing each other with their finger tips touching. Gradually, others move up from the congregation to stand beside them until there are two lines of people facing one another for the next hymn.

All: (Hymn) We are one in the Spirit.

Minister: Helen and Tony have thanked God for his promise of a child. They accept his offer with joy, in the knowledge that whatever happens will be his will, and go forward together in peace and joy to a greater happiness than they have ever known before. Let us bless God for this!

Appendix C

Welcoming People into the Hospital Congregation

All:(Hymn) All my hope on God is founded.
Minister: Help one another to carry these heavy loads, and in this way you will fulfil the Law of Christ.
Welcome to this service! The Lord be with you.
All: And also with you.
Minister: Lord Jesus Christ, behold your family gathered here, sharing a common need, united by a common hope, members of one another through our life in you. Help us to communicate the life you give us. As we participate in one another's pain, may we find courage and hope in your presence with us, whose power comes to its full strength in our weakness. Amen.

A member of the congregation reads a passage from the Old Testament (e.g. Hosea 6:1-3, 'on the third day he will restore us'). Another person - preferably one of the newcomers - reads a New Testament passage (e.g. Cor 12:1-27, 'now you are Christ's body and each of you a limb or organ of it'). Other non-biblical material may be used: it should convey something of the reality of the corporate life centred upon the hospital church or chapel. Ideally staff as well as patients would be involved here.

Minister: Sidney, Muriel, Desmond, Grace - we welcome you to St Faith's Hospital Church, and to the hospital that we serve and represent. This will be your church while you are here. In a way, of course, it will always be your church, for we hope that you will carry something of us away with you when you leave hospital. As Christians we all belong together whether we worship in great cathedrals, ancient parish churches or hospital chapels, and whatever denomination we are. This church is open to you, to come to services, or to use privately, whatever you feel like doing. Perhaps you may feel you would like to come along and spend some time here by yourself. That is what it's for. But it's also for fellowship, for being with other Christians, for sharing our joys and sorrows, our hopes and disappointments together. Being in hospital can be a frightening time, as well as a painful one. It need not be a lonely one. We are here to try to make sure it isn't. Helping one another is what Christians are for. And when we help one another we are helped ourselves. People can learn a lot about God's love in a place like this. Sometimes it takes time to sink in - but you never forget it. It can change your life.

All: (Hymn) Help us to help each other Lord.

Two or three members of the congregation lead each new member around the church or chapel building, pointing out places and objects of interest to him or her, but leaving out the altar. They can spend a few minutes in each location, and need not join in the singing, which should simply provide the background to their journey. Another hymn (We love the place, O God) may be used to allow more time. At the end of this the new members are conducted to the altar, where a hymn book or service order (or something else associated with the church) has been set aside for each of them. The minister presents them with these one at a time.

Minister: Muriel [and Sidney, Desmond and Grace] we welcome you to St Faith's and give you this sign of membership.
All: Welcome!
(Hymn) Father, Lord of all Creation.
Minister: Beloved, we have welcomed Grace, Desmond, Muriel and Sidney into the fellowship of St Faith's Church. It is a happy day for us, and we hope it is for them too. Jesus said that where two or three have gathered together in his name, he is among them. He is here with us now. Let us rejoice and give thanks.

All: (Psalms 133, 134)

Minister: Lord God, the protector of all who trust in you, without whom nothing is strong, nothing is holy: increase and multiply upon us your mercy, that you being our ruler and guide, we may so pass through things temporal that we finally lose not the things eternal. Grant this, heavenly Father, for the sake of Jesus Christ our Lord.

All: Amen.

The Lord's Prayer

The Grace of our Lord Jesus Christ, and the love of God, and the fellowship of the Holy Spirit, be with us always. Amen.

(Hymn) Hail thee, Festival Day.

Appendix D

Rite of Farewell and Encouragement

(For those leaving a psychiatric hospital to take up residence 'in the community'.)

All: (Hymn) Guide me, O thou great Redeemer.
Minister: Thy rod and thy staff comfort me.
The Lord be with you.
All: And also with you.
Minister: Every second of every minute we need your guidance, Lord God our Father. However self-confident we may be, we need your strength to support us, the knowledge of your love to encourage us. Give us, we pray, a sense of your presence with us, so that, wherever we wander, we may always know that we are at home in your love. Through Jesus Christ our Lord. Amen.

A member of the congregation reads Jonah 1 ('the sailors were afraid'). A patient who is leaving hospital reads Matt. 14:22-33 ('Jesus at once reached out and caught hold of him'). Other readings can of course be used instead, so long as they express the feelings of anxiety and uncertainty about the future. If the Jonah reading is used it could be accompanied by a mime and appropriate music.

Minister: Grahame, Joanna and Stephen are going to leave the hospital soon, and this is what our service is about today - setting out from a place you know to a new kind of life you don't know yet. We all know

this place isn't perfect. Far from it. It can be awful sometimes, but it's what we know, and where our friends are. I for one wouldn't like to leave it, and I don't actually live here. On the other hand, just think of what it might be like 'out there'. New things to do, new places to go, new opportunities, new possibilities. It might turn out to be marvellous. You never know, do you? Anyway, it's bound to be a challenge. Grahame and Stephen have lived here for a very long time, so it's really their home. They've been over to [the name of the hostel where they'll be living] and spent some time there. Joanna hasn't been in hospital for so long and she's moving into a flat on ... estate. I know that all three have been looking forward to leaving, but now the time is getting closer they begin to feel a bit nervous. This service is to give them confidence: Confidence that those of us who are still here are still their friends, still part of their lives. Confidence in the love of God to carry them wherever they are going and lay their fears to rest.
For three days and three nights Jonah remained in the sea creature's belly.
All: (Hymn) For those in peril on the sea.

The congregation line up on either side of the central aisle (if the church has one: if not, two ranks are formed in the space at the front of the church). The patients who are about to leave the hospital move up the church between the ranks, starting at the back and working forwards. As they pass along, the people on both sides greet them, in as many ways as they can think of - shaking their hands, patting them on the shoulder, hugging them, kissing them, etc. (People may need help in this, if the leavers are not to become too overwhelmed by it all.) When they have greeted the leavers the people in the two ranks close in behind them and follow them up the church, so that they end up ahead of a small crowd of people before the altar. At the altar a member of the congregation reads Jonah 2. On the line 'Then the Lord spoke to the fish and it spewed Jonah out on the dry land' all the congregation return as quickly as possible to their seats, leaving the 'Jonahs' standing before the altar.
All: (Hymn) Praise to the Holiest in the height.
Minister: Here they are, Grahame, Joanna and Stephen. Just like Jonah, on dry land again. The friendship and love they have here gives them a sure footing for the future. We have reminded them of God's love that brings us through all the dangers and difficulties, all the fears and anxieties of this life.

O Lord our God, O God our Father, thank you with our whole heart for the deliverance you send your people, and particularly for your great love shown to Stephen, Joanna and Grahame. You have opened up new ways before them and prepared them a future full of happiness. As they prepare for whatever is to come, we offer up their anxieties and doubts in union with Jesus Christ our Lord who suffered, died and rose again for our sake, and is alive and reigns with you in the unity of the Holy Spirit now and always. Amen.

All: *The Lord's Prayer*
(Psalm 16)

Minister: Jesus said: 'Courage! The victory is mine; I have conquered the world.' To God's gracious mercy and protection we commit you, Grahame, Joanna and Stephen. May the Lord bless you and watch over you. May he make his face shine upon you and give you peace; and the blessing of God almighty, the Father, Son and Holy Spirit be among you and remain with you always. Amen.

All: The grace ... evermore.
(Hymn) Will your anchor hold in the storms of life?

Appendix E

Facing an Ordeal

All: (Hymn) Father, hear the prayer we offer.
Minister: Find your strength in the Lord, in his mighty power.
Put on all the armour which God provides.
The Lord be with you.
All: And with your spirit.
Minister: Lord of our life and situation, remind us now of our weakness so that we may discover your strength and live in obedience and peace under your wing's shadow. In the name of the prince of peace, Jesus Christ our Lord.

Members of the congregation may use various ways of portraying the protagonist's present situation and feelings. Suitable bible passages, which could be read or acted, with appropriate lighting and music, would be 1 Sam. 17 (to be performed with imagination and skill!) and Eph. 6:10-20.

Minister: What we have been seeing and hearing applies to all of us at some time in our lives, perhaps more than once. Today it refers particularly to Robin. Robin has come to one of those challenging places in the course of his journey through life when there is a mountain to climb, a river to ford, a jungle to penetrate, a desert to cross, or all four, one after the other. Robin has asked us to go with him in imagination and spirit. [With Robin's permission, the minister sketches the actual situation. He tries to be as explicit as possible about the main points and to bring home the central conflict.] Robin, this is something that you have to face, certainly, but do not think you will be alone. Perhaps you will come through easily, without noticeable bruises or scars. Perhaps you won't. If you don't you may feel you have let yourself, and other people, down. Try not to feel that way. Ours is a travelling God. The journey is the thing; and today, in this place, we are with you in your journey.

Robin, are you ready to set off on your journey?

Protagonist: I am ready.

Minister: What do you carry with you?

Protagonist: I walk in Christ's Spirit and carry nothing with me.

Minister: That being so, God go with you.

All: God go with you.

(Hymn) Guide me, O Thou great Jehovah.

The events and images of this central section will be affected by the nature of the ordeal to be undergone. In the religious language of mankind, however, human ordeals are commonly symbolised geographically - as forests, torrents, icy wastes or burning deserts; or physiologically, as the belly of a monster or the body of a giant. All these ideas suggest a painful journey ending in an experience of deliverance. Skilful use of lighting and music might suggest this here. (Sibelius's Lemminkainen's Journey is a piece that comes to mind.) Perhaps the church aisle can suggest a cave or a forest. To be too explicit is to run the risk of being absurd; the slightest indication may put the idea across, because it is a very potent image for all human beings, and lies just below the surface of our awareness. Before embarking on his or her journey the protagonist says farewell to a group of friends gathered at the end of the church. The lighting comes up as he reaches the other end and stands before the altar.

All: (Hymn) One more step along the world I go.

Minister: In spirit, Robin has traversed the path that lies before him, and in spirit we have accompanied him on his way. When the time comes for him to make this journey in the world outside, we shall still be with him. He will not travel alone there any more than he did here.

The minister may (at his discretion) ask the protagonist if he or she has 'found' anything on his/her journey to take away and keep for the future? Does he or she feel that anything has changed?

All: (Psalm 27)

The Lord's Prayer

We are the Body of Christ. In the one Spirit we were all baptised into one body. Let us then pursue all that makes for peace and builds up our common life. We offer one another a sign of peace. Alleluia!

Minister: Dear Lord, behold your family gathered here together to share in the hopes and fears of one of your members. Guide him and keep him we pray. In the difficult times which lie ahead may he learn still more about you, and live in happiness and love. In the name and for the sake of Jesus, whose road was rocky and glorious.

(Other prayers may be requested.)

The God of peace, who brought again from the dead our Lord Jesus, that great shepherd of the sheep, through the blood of the eternal covenant, make you perfect in every good work to do his will, working in you that which is well-pleasing in his sight; and the blessing of God almighty, the Father, the Son and the Holy Spirit, be among you, and remain with you always. Amen.

All: (Hymn) Moses, I know you're the man.

Appendix F

A Bereavement Service

All: (Hymn) Come down O love divine.
Minister: Trust me: there are many dwelling places in my Father's house. The Lord be with you.
All: And also with you.
Minister: Lord of joy and sorrow, when you took flesh for us you brought all our pain within your immediate personal experience. When you opened wide your arms for us you embraced our turmoil and confusion giving us a strength and unity that holds us together even when our lives have fallen apart, an unseen centre to a world in turmoil. Hear our prayer now when we call to you out of the whirlwind, and grant us your peace. When thinking is agony to us, remind us of yourself. Amen.

A member of the congregation reads John 11:17-44 ('O sir, if you had only been here my brother would not have died'). Other passages should be read, both scriptural and secular, concentrating on material closely associated with the dead person, while favourite music may be played.

Minister: Six months ago Arthur died. At his funeral we asked God that he should rest in peace. I believe he has done just that. We meet today to try to comfort Joan, his widow. Since Arthur died Joan has had little peace. Life is empty without him. Sometimes she does not know what to do with herself, where to put herself. She is desolate, she is confused, she feels guilty, she feels angry. She wonders sometimes if she is going mad. She says she feels these things, and we know she does, those of us who have lost someone dearer to us than life, someone whose absence takes away any point or purpose in being alive. We cannot take her grief away or transform it into joy; we cannot give her peace. But we believe that God can do this, and that in eternity he has already done it. In the meantime there is confusion and anger and guilt and even despair - all these things because Joan loves Arthur so much and cannot bear to live without him. These are the wounds of love. They will heal and the love will blossom in a new way, one which cannot be contemplated now, because it hasn't happened yet. In the meantime, there is no confidence, only pain.

All: The Lord's Prayer
(Hymn) We will walk through the valley.

The lights are dimmed during the last verses of the hymn, and a few minutes silence are kept. After the silence, quiet music is played, which serves as the background to the voices of those who have known the dead person and who, one by one, describe what he or she was like, repeating things he or she said, describing various things he or she did. It may be possible to address some of this to the bereaved person; 'Do you remember, Joan, when you and Arthur went picking strawberries ...' 'Arthur liked that time of the year, didn't he, Joan?' This should end with somebody asking the bereaved person what hymn should be sung, 'what would Arthur like us to sing now, Joan?'
All: (Hymn) (as requested by the bereaved person)
Minister: Though separated by death, Joan and Arthur belong together. Thanks to Joan, we have been able to spend some moments in Arthur's company. Joan is always there, always in his company. As God is with her always and Arthur is with him. And we are here with you Joan, until the morning comes, the landscape lightens, and you move on your way.
All: Benedictus: Blessed be the Lord God of Israel ... for ever and ever. Amen.
Minister: Lord Jesus Christ, we commend Joan to you now, in this stage of her journeying. We ask you to comfort and bless her, offering up on her behalf all her longings and desires, feelings and thoughts, confusions and certainties, and the things she dare not think, to you in the name and for the sake of him who wept for Lazarus at the tomb, Jesus Christ our Lord.
All: Come, Lord Jesus.

The minister encourages members of the congregation to embrace the bereaved person. Perhaps a cup of tea might be served before the last hymn.

All: (Hymn) My God loves me.
Minister: Grant, O Father, that we may be reunited in the full knowledge of your love and the unclouded   vision of your glory; through Jesus Christ our Lord, Amen.

Notes

Introduction

1. Grainger, R. *The Language of the Rite*. Darton, Longman & Todd, 1974.
2. cf. Goulder, M. *Midrash and Lection in Matthew*, SPCK, 1974. Guilding, A. *The Fourth Gospel in Recent Criticism*, Oxford University Press, 1960; Trocmé, E. *The Passion as Liturgy*. SCM, 1984; also Douglas, M. *Purity and Danger*, Routledge, 1966; and Meeks, W. *The First Urban Christians*, Yale University, New Haven, 1982.

Chapter 1

1. Quoted in Toffler, A. *Future Shock*, p.22. Pan, 1971.
2. Perls, S.F., Hefferline, R.F. and Goodman, P. *Gestalt Therapy*. Penguin, 1973. The authors claim that the effect of the struggle to achieve cognitive consistency is in fact disturbed emotional stasis, emotion itself being 'a critical state of perception'.
3. Tillich, P. *The Courage to Be*, p.71. Collins, 1952.
4. Buber, M. *I and Thou*, p.40. T & T Clark, Edinburgh, 1966.
5. Geertz, C. 'Religion as a Cultural System', in M. Banton (ed.), *Anthropological Approaches to the Study of Religion*, p.14. Tavistock, 1966.
6. Berger, J. *The Social Reality of Religion*, p.28. Penguin, 1973.
7. Berger, J. *The Social Reality of Religion*, p.46.
8. Gluckman, M. *Essays on the Ritual of Social Relationships*. Manchester University Press, 1962. Gluckman points out that those times of spiritual communion that we associate with corporate worship by no means always reflect a condition of harmony in the ordinary social life of the participants.
9. Jung's account of the universality of religion at the level of the 'collective unconscious' may seem to make it less than personal. Viktor Frankl warns that 'the unconscious God' must not be mistaken as an impersonal force operant in man. Jung, however, is describing the level of psychic reality underlying our unique individual experiences of God and the personal decisions we make as a result of them. (Frankl, V. *The Unconscious God*, p.62. Hodder & Stoughton, 1975.)
10. Jung, C.G. *Psychology and Religion*, p.92. Yale University, New Haven, 1938.
11. McGuire, W. and Hull, R.F.C. (eds) *C.G. Jung Speaking*, p.328. Thames & Hudson, 1978.

12. Jacobi, J. *The Psychology of C.G. Jung*, p.131. Routledge, 1962.

13. McGuire, W. and Hull, R.F.C. *(eds) C.G. Jung Speaking*, p.327. Thames & Hudson, 1978.

14. 'anomie ... springs from the lack of collective forces at certain points on society: that is, of groups established for the regulation of social life' (Durkheim, E. *Suicide. A Study in Sociology*, trans. J.A. Spaulding and G. Simpson, pp.382-406. RKP, 1952.)

15. The practice of bestowing a name at baptism is a comparatively late (and liturgically doubtful) aevelopment within liturgical tradition (See Fisher, J.D.C. *Christian Initiation: Baptism in the Medieval West*. SPCK, 1965.) and one that has led to distress in situations where people who already possessed a personal name have been required to assume another one as the pledge of their willingness to be baptised. In the case of infants, the problem does not exist, but adult baptism, which is regaining its original place as the preferred method, may give rise to serious problems if a new name has to be assumed by the candidate: 'A name which is inherited from one's original culture roots the baptised in that culture, and at the same time manifests the universality of baptism, incorporation into the one Church, holy catholic and apostolic, which stretches over all the nations of the earth.' (Lima Ecumenical Statement on Baptism.)

16. Laurentin, A. 'Theatre and Liturgy', in *Worship*, 43, 404, 1969. Collegeville, Minnesota.

17. Balasuriya, T. *The Eucharist and Human Liberation*. SCM, 1979.

18. Grainger, R. *The Language of the Rite*. Darton, Longman & Todd, 1974.

Chapter 2

1. cf. Wilson, B.R. (ed.) *Patterns of Sectarianism*. Heinemann, 1967.

2. Clare, A. *Psychiatry in Dissent*, p.210. Tavistock, 1976.

3. Douglas, M. *Natural Symbols*, ch.3. Penguin, 1973.

4. Wilson, M. *The Hospital: A Place of Truth*. Birmingham University, 1971.

5. Revens, R.W. *Standards for Morale, xvi*. Oxford University Press, 1964.

6. Speck, P. *Loss and Grief in Medicine*, pp.6,7. Ballière Tindall, 1978.

7. Grainger, R. 'The social symbolism of grief and mourning' (Ph.D. thesis). Leeds University, 1971.

8. Freud, S. *The Future of an Illusion*, p.26. Hogarth Press, 1970.

9. Indeed, Jung quarrelled with Freud on this very point: symbols were not to be regarded as ways of disguising emotion, but as the only appropriate channel of communication for thoughts and feelings associated with the kind of experiencing in which emotion, driven by the need to express itself as clearly and directly as possible, actually creates its own kind of language - one which gives an infinite resonance to the literal description of persons, places and events. 'I had the idea that certain things are symbolical [of a wider truth than the individual's current psychological state]. Freud would not agree to this, and he identified his method with the theory and the theory with the method.' (See Jung, C.G. *Analytical*

Psychology, p.140. Routledge, 1968.)

10. 'The legend of the Shade which appears and demands the burial of its bones ... forms part of mankind's permanent heritage' (Lovecraft, H.P. *Supernatural Horror in Literature*, p.19. Dover, New York, 1973.) cf. Bendann, E. *Death Customs*, Kegan Paul, 1930; Frazer, J.G. *The Fear of the Dead in Primitive Religion*, Macmillan, 1933; Habenstein, R.W. and Lamers, W.M. *Funeral Customs the World Over*, Bulfin, Milwaukee, 1963; Puckle, B.S. *Funeral Customs, their Origin and Development*, T. Werner Lawrie, London, 1926.

11. Luckman, T. *The Invisible Religion*. Macmillan, 1967.

Chapter 3

1. Jung, C.G. *Psychology and Religion*, p.57. Yale University, New Haven, 1938.

2. Eliade, M. *Rites and Symbols of Initiation*, p.112. Harper & Row, 1965.

3. Hameline, J-Y. 'Relire van Gennep; les rites de passage', in *La maison Dieu*. Paris, 112, 1972. pp.133-43

4. Weiner, N. *Cybernetics or Control and Communication in the Animal and the Machine*, pp.145, 146. MIT, Cambridge, Mass., 1961.

5. Claridge, G. *The Origins of Mental Illness*, p.47. Blackwell, 1985.

Chapter 4

1. Gennep, A. van *The Rites of Passage*, trans. M.B. Vizedom and G.L. Caffee, p.189. Routledge, 1960.

2. Gennep, A. van *The Rites of Passage*, trans. M.B. Vizedom and G.L. Caffee, p.10. Routledge, 1960.

3. Gorman, C. *The Book of Ceremony*, p.45. Whole Earth Tools, Cambridge, 1972.

4. Eliade, M. *Rites and Symbols of Initiation*, p.31. Harper & Row, 1965.

5. Reformed theology has played its part: 'Where the tree falls, there let it lie!'

6. Eph. 4:13.

7. Eph. 6:12.

8. Masson, C. *L'Epître de Saint Paul aux Ephésiens*, CNT, Neuchatel, 1953.

9. Noakes, K.W. 'Initiation from New Testament times until St Cyprian', in C. Jones, C. Wainwright and E. Yarnold (eds) *The Study of Liturgy*, p.91f. SPCK, 1979.

10. Burnish, R. *The Meaning of Baptism*. Alcuin, SPCK, 1986. Burnish compares the teaching and practices of the fourth century with those of today; cf. also Kelly, J.N.D. *Early Christian Doctrines*. A & C Black, 1958.

11. Hauerwas, S. and Bondi, R. *Truthfulness and Tragedy*. University of Notre Dame, Indiana, 1977.

12. Turner, V.W. *The Ritual Process*, p.8. Penguin, 1974.

13. Ghibran, K. *The Prophet*, pp.16, 19. Heinemann, 1923.

14. This constitutes the first ten sections of the ASB service and the 'Entrance Rite',

'Liturgy of the Word' and 'Consent' in the Rite of Marriage for use in the Dioceses of England and Wales.

15. Parkes, C.M. *Bereavement: Studies of Grief in Adult Life*, Tavistock, 1972; and Bowlby, J. *Attachment and Loss*, vol III, Penguin, 1981.

16. Malinowski, B. *Magic, Science and Religion*. Souvenir Press, 1974.

17. 'Judging by my interviews and the range of rituals and practices reported by historians and anthropologists, it would seem as though most adult mourners pass through three stages - (1) a period of shock, usually between the occurrence of the death and the disposal of the body, (2) a period of intense mourning, accompanied by withdrawal of much attention from the external world and by such psychological changes as disturbed and restless sleep, often with vivid dreams, failure of appetite and loss of weight, (3) a final period of re-established physical homeostasis, sleep and weight again established, interest again directed outwards.' (Gorer, G. *Death, Grief and Mourning in Contemporary Britain*, p.112. Cresset, 1965.)

18. Eliade, M. *Myths, Dreams and Mysteries*, p.41. Collins, 1968.

19. Isa. 14:18, 19.

20. van Gennep, A. *The Rites of Passage*, p.160. Routledge, 1960.

21. Habenstein, R.W. and Lamers, W.M. *Funeral Customs the World Over*. Bulfin, Milwaukee, 1963.

Chapter 5

1. Kavanagh, A. *The Shape of Baptism: The Rite of Christian Initiation*, p.120. Pueblo, New York, 1978.

2. 2 Peter 3:9.

3. John 13:8.

4. Matt. 10:39, 16:25; Mark 8:35; Luke 9:24.

5. Col. 3:11.

6. Matt. 25:40.

7. cf. Phil. 2:6-11 and Rom. 8:29.

8. Rom. 8:30.

9. 1 Cor. 15:53-56.

10. Turner, V.W. *The Ritual Process*, pp.119-54. Penguin, 1974.

11. Cox, H. *The Secular City*. SCM, 1965.

12. cf. Col. 2:15. St Paul seems to have associated the idea of Satanic powers with the demonic aspect of Jewish legalism, the process whereby works (the structures of human thought and action) are substituted for faith (the relationship of persons through which they achieve personhood); cf. Caird, G.B. *Principalities and Powers*, p.4. Oxford University Press, 1956. 'When the law is isolated and exalted into an independent system of religion it becomes demonic. This corruption of the law is the work of sin, in particular the sin of self-righteousness'. Self-righteousness and the idolatry of human institutions appear to be much the same thing, the latter being a corporate version of the former.

BIBLIOGRAPHY

Balasuriya, T. *The Eucharist and Human Liberation*, SCM, London, 1979

Bailey, E. (Ed.) *A Workbook in Popular Religion*, Partners,Dorchester, 1986

Banton, M. *Anthropological Approaches to the Study of Religion*, Tavistock, London, 1966

Bendann, E. *Death Customs*, Kegan Paul, London, 1930

Berger, P. *The Social Reality of Religion*, Penguin, London, 1973

Buber, M. *I and Thou*, T. & T. Clark, Edinburgh, 1966

Burnish, R. *The Meaning of Baptism*, Alcuin/SPCK, London, 1986

Caird, G.B. *Principalities and Powers*, OUP, Oxford, 1956

Clare, A. *Psychiatry in Dissent*, Tavistock, London, 1976

Claridge, G. *The Origins of Mental Illness*, Blackwell, Oxford, 1985

Cox, H. *The Secular City*, SCM,London, 1965

Douglas, M. *Purity and Danger*, RKP, London, 1966

Eliade, M. *Rites and Symbols of Initiation*, Harper & Row, London, 1965
     Myths, Dreams and Mysteries, Collins, London, 1968

Fisher, J.D.C. *Christian Initiation: Baptism in the Medieval West*, SPCK, London, 1965

Frankl, V. *The Unconscious God*, Hodder & Stoughton, London 1975

Frazer, J.G. *The Fear of Death in Primitive Religion*, Macmillan, London, 1933

Freud, S. *The Future of an Illusion*, Hogarth, London, 1970

Gennep, A. van *The Rites of Passage* (Trans. M.B. Vizedom and G.L. Caffee), Routledge, London, 1960

Ghibran, K. *The Prophet*, Heinemann, London, 1923

Gluckman, M. *Essays on the Ritual of Social Relationships*, University Press, Manchester, 1962

Gorer, C. *Death, Grief and Mourning in Contemporary Britain*, Cresset, London 1965

Gorman, C. *The Book of Ceremony*, Whole Earth Tools, Cambridge, 1972

Goulder, M. *Midrash and Lection in Matthew*, SPCK, London, 1974

Grainger, R. *The Language of the Rite*, Darton, Longman & Todd, London, 1974
     Watching for Wings, Darton, Longman & Todd, London, 1979
          'The Social Symbolism of Grief and Mourning', (Ph.D thesis) Leeds University, Leeds, 1979
          'The Funeral as a Work of Art', *New Blackfriars*, Oxford (1980) 61, 181-185, 719

'The Language of Ritual', *ibid* (1983) 64, 757, 325-330

'Ritual and Agnosticism', *ibid* (1984) 65, 764, 63-68

'The Sacraments as Passage Rites', *Worship*, Collegeville (1984) 58, 3, 214-221

'What's in a Name?', *New Fire*, Oxford (1984) VII, 58, 30-34

Guilding, A. *The Fourth Gospel in Recent Criticism*, OUP, Oxford, 1960

Habenstein, R.W. & Lamers, W.M. *Funeral Customs the World Over*, Bulfin, Milwaukee, 1963

Hameline, J-Y., '*Relire van Gennep; les Rites de Passage*', La Maison Dieu, Paris (1972) 112, 133-143

Hauerwas, S. & Bondi, R. *Truthfulness and Tragedy*, University of Notre Dame, Notre Dame, Indiana, 1977

Jacobi, J. *The Psychology of C.G. Jung*, RKP, London, 1962

Jones, C., Wainwright, G., & Yarnold, E. (Eds) *The Study of Liturgy*, SPCK, London, 1979

Jung, C.G. *Psychology and Religion*, Yale, New Haven, 1938
        Analytical Psychology, RKP, London, 1968

Kavanagh, A. *The Shape of Baptism: The Rite of Christian Initiation*, Pueblo, New York, 1978

Kelly, J.N.D. *Early Christian Doctrines*, A. & C. Black, London, 1958

Laurentin, A. 'Theatre and Liturgy', *Worship*, Collegeville, Minnesota 1969 7, 43, 382-406

Lovecraft, H.P. *Supernatural Horror in Literature*, Dover, New York, 1973

Luckman, T. *The Invisible Religion*, Macmillan, London, 1967

McGuire, W. & Hull R.F.C. (Eds) *C.G. Jung Speaking*, Thames & Hudson, London, 1978

Malinowski, B. *Magic, Science and Religion*, Souvenir Press, London, 1974

Masson, C., *L'Epître de Saint Paul aux Ephésiens*, ENT, Neuchatel, 1953

Meeks, W. *The First Urban Christians*, Yale, New Haven, 1982

Moss, T. *In Search of Christianity*, Firethorn, London, 1986

Perls, S.F., Hefferline, R.F. & Goodman, P. *Gestalt Therapy*, Penguin, London, 1973

Puckle, B.S. *Funeral Customs, their Origin and Development*, London, 1926

Revens, R.W. *Standards for Morale*, OUP, Oxford, 1964

Speck, P. *Loss and Grief in Medicine*, Baillière Tindall, London, 1978

Tillich, P. *The Courage to Be*, Collins, London, 1952

Toffler, A. *Future Shock*, Pan, London, 1971

Trocmé, E. *The Passion as Liturgy*, SCM, London, 1984

Turner, V.W. *The Ritual Process*, Penguin, London, 1974

Weiner, N. *Cybernetics, or Control and Communication in the Animal and the Machine*, MIT, Cambridge (Mass), 1961

Wilson, B.R. (Ed) *Patterns of Sectarianism*, Heinemann, London, 1967

Wilson, M. *The Hospital - A Place of Truth*, University of Birmingham, Birmingham, 1971

Index